THE
HIGHLAND
RAILWAY

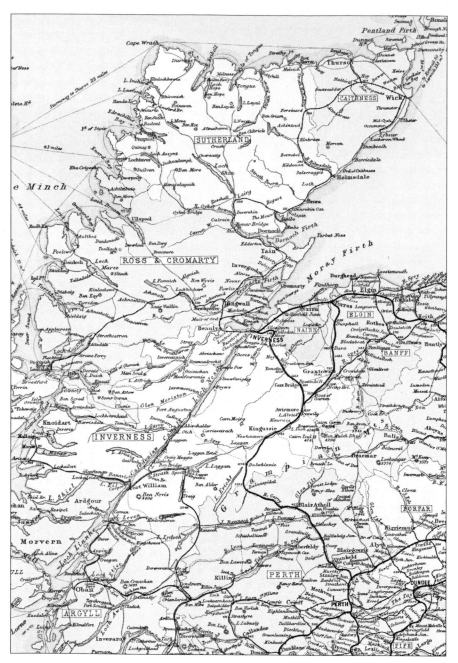

The Highland Railway from Bartholomew's Survey Atlas of Scotland, 1912.
(Reproduced by permission of the Trustees of the National Library of Scotland)

THE
HIGHLAND
RAILWAY

KEITH FENWICK AND HOWARD GEDDES

The History Press

Conon was a station on the line north from Inverness, one stop before Dingwall. Its staff, shown here in 1920, was typical of a wayside station on the Highland Railway and consisted of a stationmaster, porter, clerk and two porters/pointsmen. The station closed in 1960, but plans are now in hand to open one nearby to serve modern housing developments. (Scottish Railway Preservation Society)

First published 2009
Reprinted 2010, 2011, 2012

The History Press
The Mill, Brimscombe Port
Stroud, Gloucestershire, GL5 2QG
www.thehistorypress.co.uk

ISBN 978 0 7509 5094 7

Typesetting and origination by The History Press
Printed and bound in Great Britain by
Marston Book Services Limited, Didcot

CONTENTS

INTRODUCTION

There have been plenty of books on the Highland Railway over the years; Hamilton Ellis' *Highland Engines and Their Work* in the 1920s, H.A. Vallance's *History of the Highland Railway* in the 1930s, M.C.V. Allchin's work on the Highland locomotives in the 1940s, the Stephenson Locomotive Society's Centenary book of 1954, which was packed with facts, and O.S. Nock's *Highland Railway* of 1965 have all made notable contributions. Anthony Lambert and Peter Tatlow have contributed photographic albums while David Hunter and Neil T. Sinclair have added more detailed studies, and J.L. Stevenson and Revd Cormack produced the final word on locomotives. Liveries have been covered in depth by Eddie Bellass and Howard Geddes. The Regional History series has naturally covered the lines and, recently, David Ross has taken a new look at the history of the company itself. To this list must be added all the albums which have included Highland lines and the wealth of articles which have appeared in magazines over the years.

So why another book? This one is an album, which by definition can only provide a snapshot of the subject. It cannot present a complete story, but we have tried to give a flavour of the Highland and explore some of its more interesting aspects. We have also brought the story up to date, as the railway continues to adapt to modern needs.

We start by describing the area served by the Highland Railway, followed by four chapters chronicling the development of the system. We then look at locomotives, rolling stock, structures and signalling, continuing on to that inevitable subject, the weather. To conclude we look at a few survivors and see how the railway today continues to serve its customers.

Our thanks go to all the photographers who have contributed to this book, particularly the Highland Railway Society (HRS), who allowed us to use pictures from its collection. Each photograph is credited individually where the source or photographer is known.

We hope that these pages will inspire you to visit the area, model some aspect of it or just enjoy its rich scenery and history in print.

Keith Fenwick and Howard Geddes, 2009

1

WHAT MAKES THE HIGHLAND DIFFERENT?

The Highland Railway stretched from Perth via Inverness to Wick and Thurso, a distance of over 278 miles, or a bit more than that from London to Newcastle-upon-Tyne. The centre of the system was Inverness, the capital of the Highlands and by far the largest town north of Aberdeen. The development of Inverness and the Highland Railway in the second half of the nineteenth century go hand-in-hand; the town depended on the railway to link it to the outside world and the railway provided employment for a significant portion of its workforce. The railway was controlled and financed by the Highland lairds who looked on Inverness as their main town.

But the railway served more than just Inverness: it provided the largely rural population with all its needs. It took sheep and cattle to market and it brought in coal, supplies and tourists.

Inverness was a difficult town to reach. The direct approach from the south had to find a way from Perth through the Cairngorm mountains, but the easier route via Aberdeen was much longer. In fact, the Aberdeen line was completed first, but control was split between two companies so it was not long before the railway to Perth was built. This presented a challenge to Victorian railway engineers and has ever since made the life of the operating department difficult, especially in the thick of a winter storm. Then the railway expanded northwards, eventually reaching Wick and Thurso in the far north. This was an easier route, going along or near the coast for much of the journey, but the final portion had to go inland to avoid the coastal cliffs.

The other significant line ran from Dingwall to the west coast. This is the fabled Kyle of Lochalsh line, built to connect with steamers to Skye and the Western Isles and nowadays providing one of the most enjoyable tourist journeys in the country.

All these lines covered considerable distances. Along the coast north of Inverness and eastwards towards Aberdeen, the country was fairly well populated and various towns provided healthy intermediate traffic. But both the main line to Perth and the Kyle line traversed sparsely populated countryside. One could travel for many miles and see little more than the occasional croft.

Several branch lines were built, their short trains and tank engines contrasting with the larger tender engines and substantial trains on the main lines. All these branches have long been closed, as has part of the original main line north of Aviemore, but the main routes still operate, meeting the essential needs of the Highlanders and as popular as ever with tourists. There is still much to be enjoyed, not least the incomparable scenery.

The Highland Railway carried on a profitable business by matching its services closely to demand. Passenger traffic surged in summer as the tourists arrived. The high-point was always the Glorious Twelfth, 12 August, the start of grouse shooting, when half of London society decamped to the Highlands of Scotland, made popular by Queen Victoria in the 1840s. Goods traffic was more evenly spread over the year, but each spring and autumn special trains carried sheep to and from their summer grazing in the higher ground of the Grampians and north of Inverness.

Modern comforts were only introduced slowly. Lavatories appeared in the early years of the twentieth century, but it was the second decade before steam heating was introduced on the long run to Wick and Thurso, just the sort of route which should have benefitted many years earlier given the grim winter conditions.

To work these trains, the company built a succession of distinctive locomotives. The Crewe front end with inclined cylinders was favoured in the 1870s and '80s. To handle goods traffic over the steep gradients between Perth and Inverness, the country's first 4-6-0s were introduced in 1894. Further 4-6-0 classes followed to power the main trains, while the older 4-4-0s survived on lesser duties and piloting their larger successors. Branches were operated by a variety of tank locomotives.

Change came gradually to the railway after the grouping in 1923, when it became part of the London, Midland & Scottish Railway (LMS). Newer coaches made an early appearance but it was not until the mid-1930s that Stanier's Black Fives provided really capable motive power. The LMS continued to develop services on the main lines but trimmed back several of the branches where buses served local needs much more effectively. Even so, operating the lines north of Inverness became less attractive and the LMS examined the possibility of shutting them down.

As with many other parts of the country, the early years of British Railways (BR) saw little change. The Highlands were one of the first areas to be completely dieselised, with little steam operation after 1960. Dr Beeching's clean sweep posed the first serious threat by proposing closure of all the lines north of Inverness, together with many of the local stations on the remaining routes to Perth and Aberdeen. In the event, only the original main line north from Aviemore to Forres was closed, along with local stations. However, the fate of the Kyle line was again in doubt when permission was given in 1971 to close it in 1974. The arrival of the North Sea oil industry stopped that from happening and brought additional freight traffic to parts of the system for several years.

Most freight died off by the mid-1990s, but improvements to the passenger services have continued thanks to the subsidies now available. The main lines from Perth and Aberdeen to Inverness and then on to Wick, Thurso and Kyle remain open and now enjoy a better service than ever before. Growing traffic congestion in Inverness, now a bustling city, has led to the re-introduction of local trains from Kingussie and Invergordon. The old manual and labour-intensive signalling gave way to radio control north of Inverness in the 1980s and modern diesel multiple units replaced locomotive haulage; these steps have helped to keep subsidies to tolerable levels.

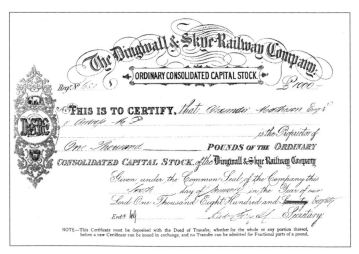

The Dingwall & Skye Railway crossed the country north of Inverness and was built to open up routes to Skye and the Western Isles. Still open today, passenger trains are heavily subsidised but provide one of the most enjoyable railway journeys in the country. Alexander Matheson, who had made his fortune working for Jardine Matheson in Hong Kong, was a major landowner in the area and strong backer of the Highland Railway. He was chairman of the company throughout its existence from 1865 to 1880 and chairman of the Highland from its formation in 1865 until 1884, having previously been chairman of the Inverness & Aberdeen Junction and deputy chairman of the Inverness & Perth Junction Railways. (HRS collection)

2
ROUTES

Apart from the scenery, the distance and sparse population are significant in understanding how the Highland Railway developed. From Inverness, it was 144 miles to Perth by the original route and 117 miles after the direct line from Aviemore was opened. To Keith it is 55 miles, Wick 161 miles and 81 miles to Kyle of Lochalsh.

The line eastward to Keith serves three significant towns, Nairn, Forres and Elgin. There are towns and villages dotted along the east coast as far as Helmsdale on the line to the far north, but its last 60 miles now serve nowhere in particular. The one town on the Kyle route, Strathpeffer, had to be bypassed because of the objections of the local landowner. Neither Strome Ferry, the original terminus, nor Kyle of Lochalsh were anything more than railheads for the connecting ferry services to Skye and the Outer Isles. Even the main line south to Perth passes through some pretty barren country; Grantown, Kingussie, Pitlochry and Dunkeld were the only towns of any significance when the line was built.

The main line from Perth to Inverness presented the operating department with a considerable challenge. In the northbound direction, the summit of Druimuachdar was 1,484ft above sea level and involved a climb of several miles at 1 in 70. The wild nature of the country is well illustrated in this view of a southbound train hauled by a Jones Big Goods near the summit. The Big Goods were the first 4-6-0s in the British Isles and were specifically designed to handle goods trains on this route without double heading. (HRS collection)

The summit of Druimuachdar (pronounced Drum-OCH-ter). Double track was installed on the steep climb up from Blair Atholl at the beginning of the twentieth century. Inset is the early BR version of the summit sign. This view is looking north, with the summit sign on the far left, 1937. (HRS collection)

The population of Inverness grew in the first half of the nineteenth century from 8,000 to 16,000 and it was the administrative and social centre for the whole of the Highlands in a period when clan influences were still strong. Its comparative isolation made it self-sufficient and the people followed their own ways. All that would change once the railway arrived.

Despite the distance involved, Inverness was the objective of various proposals during the railway mania of the mid-1840s. Inverness interests, backed by the expertise of Joseph Mitchell (who in due course engineered the early lines), wanted to go south through the Grampian hills to Perth, but a more practical way was via Aberdeen. Parliament thought the Grampian route too difficult for the locomotives of the day and so approved the route to Aberdeen, but Inverness folk would not contribute to a line they could not control. In the event, it took several years to begin construction of the Great North of Scotland Railway (GNSR) and after the first section, from Aberdeen to Huntly, was opened in 1854, powers to carry on had expired. This enabled the promotion of the first part of what was to become the Highland Railway, the Inverness & Nairn, opened in 1855. Over the next few years, the two railways were extended to meet at Keith, the through route being completed in August 1858.

Relations with the GNSR were never good, so plans for the line from Forres via Grantown, Kingussie and Pitlochry to Dunkeld, where it connected with an existing line from Perth, were revived and the line promoted in 1860. After a remarkably short construction time, it was opened in 1863, a bit too late for the tourist season of that year and a bit too early to allow proper preparation to be made. It took a few months for the staff, many of whom knew nothing about railways, to operate the line properly.

Even before the main line to Perth had opened, expansion northwards had started. Beyond Inverness, the population was generally concentrated along the coast, where people earned their living through fishing and farming. As the larger populations in the east were mainly concentrated along the coast, the main route north from Inverness kept close to the sea as much as possible.

The first section to be opened was between Inverness and Dingwall, even then an important town, in 1862. The line was extended to Invergordon the following year and then on to Bonar Bridge in 1864. Here the track had to go inland as the Dornoch Firth presented too much of an obstacle. As can be seen from the map on page 2, the route northwards was by no means direct.

Separate companies were involved in the building of these railways, but in practice the directors, backers and management were the same, so in 1865 they came together as the Highland Railway. Most of the finance for the company had come from local landowners, several of whom became board members. The Highland's board contained a high proportion of titled people and board meetings took place as often in London as in Inverness.

The Highland Railway continued expansion northwards, although this proved progressively more difficult as the population became thinner and the physical obstacles greater. After the extension to Golspie in 1868, the Highland was not keen to promote further progress northwards, but the Duke of Sutherland, one of the most important landowners in the north, had the benefit of extensive revenues from the Staffordshire coal field and bore most of the cost. The Duke of Sutherland's Railway took the line on to Helmsdale in 1871. Support from other landowners enabled completion to Wick and Thurso in 1874.

The railway to the west coast, to serve the Western Isles, had local backing, but the Highland was not happy with its financial prospects. Direct steamer services to Glasgow could just as easily meet the needs of the islanders. Still, the line was promoted and reached the west coast at Strome Ferry in 1870. The extension to Kyle of Lochalsh did not come until 1897.

A northbound train passes through Dalnaspidal, not far from the summit at Druimuachdar, in the late 1920s. The locomotive is Clan No. 14764 *Clan Munro*, but the train is a veritable mixture. From the front the coaches are: North British, Midland or LNER (ex-Midland & North British Joint), L&NW, West Coast Joint or L&NW diner, L&NW, Highland, LMS and finally Midland. LNER coaches would have come through from Edinburgh Waverley via Glenfarg. Some of the others would have come through from Glasgow, with the remainder added at Perth. The LMS transferred coaches from other parts of its system to provide better facilities on the ex-Highland section. (HRS collection)

The flat countryside from Inverness to Elgin presented little difficulty to railway builders, but the hillier section on to Keith involved heavier earthworks and a major bridge over the River Spey. This view was taken just south of Orton and looks towards Keith. On the right can be seen the trackbed of the short-lived Morayshire Railway line to Rothes. The bridge over the Spey is on the left in the distance. This was originally built in 1858 as an inverted 'U', gaining its structural strength from high box-section sides. Its construction was fraught with set-backs. The designer, a distinguished engineer of the day, crossed swords with the Board of Trade inspector over the adequacy of the iron work. It was rebuilt in 1906 as a Pratt truss bridge. (HRS collection)

By the 1880s, there was a threat to the Highland's prosperity through the promotion of a railway from Glasgow via Rannoch Moor to serve Fort William and then run up the Great Glen to Inverness. To counter this, the Highland promoted a direct line from Aviemore to Inverness via Slochd. As well as saddling the company with its capital cost, revenue was reduced because of the shorter distance. As a result, the early years of the twentieth century were ones of financial stringency for the company.

Several branches were constructed. Aberfeldy and Burghead were early ones, while those to Buckie, Fort George and Strathpeffer dated from the 1880s and '90s. The Dornoch and Lybster branches were light railways, built in the early twentieth century. There were several other proposals for light railways, mainly to serve the north west, but one, from Conon to Cromarty, was under construction when the First World War broke out; this brought progress to a stop, never to be resumed. A branch to Findhorn, never actually part of the Highland, was opened in 1860 and closed in 1869. Many of the branches succumbed to road competition in the 1930s but the Dornoch branch survived until 1960 and that to Aberfeldy, which had been the first to open, was the last to close in 1965. The original line from Aviemore to Forres also closed in 1965, but all the other lines remain open; arguably a larger proportion of the Highland's track remains than of any other pre-grouping railway.

Inverness station grew from a simple terminal to a complex triangular layout with a vast area covered by railway facilities. This view was taken in 1970 from the cab of a train heading northwards on the avoiding line, usually known as the Rose Street Curve. The former Lochgorm Works can be seen in the centre of this photograph and the passenger station on the left. The goods sidings were to the right, as was Needlefield Carriage Works.

Today, the whole area of the locomotive shed has been redeveloped as a shopping centre and supermarket. The trackwork has been simplified and colour-light signalling installed, but the lines to the station and towards the far north line are still in use. Lochgorm Works are used for maintenance of the class 158s on lines from Inverness. A facility for servicing First ScotRail's sleeping cars has been built on the site of the carriage sheds on the right; a class 08 shunter is retained at Inverness to shunt the Caledonian sleeper stock. In 2008, a new freight facility for Inverness was built on the area off to the right, which will hopefully spearhead a revival of freight traffic. (Keith Fenwick)

The Highland Railway issued tickets for all sorts of purposes. These examples enabled the good folk of Elgin and Forres to travel to Nairn to enjoy the seaside there. The outward half (right-hand side) was white with a blue circle, while the return half was salmon. The horizontal line was red. (Courtesy of John Roake)

Arguably the finest scenery on the Highland and possibly even in the whole country is to be found on the Kyle line. On a fine day, the bleak scenery of Achnasheen gives way to the tranquil waters of Loch Carron and then, as the train approaches Kyle of Lochalsh, there are spectacular views of Skye, Raasay and several other smaller islands. The line is therefore the destination of many tourists and attracts special trains from all parts of Britain. Here a returning excursion is headed by two class 37s near the head of Loch Carron. (Keith Fenwick)

Finding a route for the final stretch to Kyle of Lochalsh was not easy and involved several embankments and cuttings blasted through the rock. The tortuous nature of the line gives good views, not only looking out to sea but also of the train itself. This is a returning excursion from Aberdeen hauled by two class 37s and formed of Scottish Railway Preservation Society (SRPS) stock in August 2003. (Keith Fenwick)

The sea was never far away from much of the Highland system. Before the railways came, coastal steamers had dramatically improved access to many areas and the sea routes continued to offer competitive service for many classes of goods, particularly coal. Later, the railway ran in conjunction with sea routes to Skye and the Western Isles and that was the primary reason for building the line from Dingwall. The line was subsequently extended to the more convenient terminus of Kyle of Lochalsh in 1897. This is MacBrayne's paddle steamer *Lovedale* moured at the newly completed pier. The Highland did operate its own ships in the 1870s, but found the business unprofitable and sold out to David MacBrayne. (HRS collection)

The early morning train from Inverness has just arrived at Kyle of Lochalsh. The coaches are being unloaded and the loco is already engaged in shunting on one of the sidings on the pier. A ship passes by on its way south, February 1980. (Keith Fenwick)

Black Fives were by now the mainstay of the services but older engines, such as 54409 *Ben Alisky*, could still be seen providing assistance. This Ben was withdrawn seven months later. Here it is seen pulling the morning train from Inverness to Wick and Thurso climbing up between Kinbrace and Forsinard, September 1949. (HRS collection)

At Helmsdale, the Far North line turned inwards and ran up the Strath of Kildonan. This was not a climb to rival Slochd or Druimuachdar, but after the relative ease of the run up the coast, it made the fireman work a bit harder. Here a Black Five is seen arriving with a southbound train. On the left is the engine shed. After the closure of the Dornoch branch in 1960, the two Western Region pannier tanks were here for a while and used for shunting. (HRS collection)

Thurso, on the north coast, and Wick, on the east coast, were the two objectives of the Far North line. About 21 miles apart, it would have been easy to serve them both if the line could have run all the way up the east coast to Wick first. But the cliffs to the north of Helmsdale were too much of an obstacle and the inland route brought the line to Georgemas Junction, where a branch ran to Thurso. Trains carried portions for both towns until recent years but now, to cut costs, the train runs into Thurso and returns to Georgemas before continuing to Wick.

This view was taken in the early years of the twentieth century and shows the southbound afternoon train on the left getting ready to depart; the 1910 timetable shows trains crossing here between 3.10 p.m. and 3.18 p.m. The Thurso branch goes off to the right; it made a trailing junction to the main line which helped the marshalling of trains. The branch engine, Yankee Tank No. 54, is taking water prior to working to Thurso with the coaches which have arrived from Inverness. (HRS collection)

The same procedures were followed in 1968. Here the southbound train is being combined. The loco and three coaches, one of them a miniature buffet car, have come in from Wick and stopped by the up starter, which is already 'off', while the Thurso portion has come in on the branch track, seen in the

centre, run through the station and is backing onto the Wick portion. The shunter is leaning out of the leading door to guide the driver. Down trains were easier to handle, as they were simply divided in the down platform. Once the Wick portion had departed, the branch engine could back onto the Thurso portion and take it away. (Norris Forrest/GNSRA)

Yankee Tank No. 15013 enters Wick in LMS days with a mixed train from Lybster, illustrating the classic Highland branch line train. A single coach suffices for the traffic on that line, whose terminus was the furthest point on the LMS system from London. Henry Casserley recorded that he obtained a return ticket from London to Lybster for his first extensive tour of the old Highland Railway in 1929 and, when he presented this at St Pancras, the ticket collector merely remarked that he had a 'long way to go'; it is remarkable that he knew where Lybster was. (Author's collection)

0-4-4T No. 53 *Lybster* shunting at Wick in 1912. This loco had been rebuilt from 0-4-4ST *Strathpeffer* in 1890. Apart from at Inverness and Perth, shunting was often performed by locos between other duties. (HRS collection)

0-4-4T No. 46 and the directors' saloon have stopped at Granish Moor near Boat of Garten to allow an inspection party to descend. The men are all well dressed, several with winged collars, indicating an inspection of some importance, 20 July 1908. (HRS collection)

In the 1880s, the Highland was forced to put forward the direct line from Aviemore to Inverness to head off competition from a shorter route from Glasgow to Inverness via Fort William. It only reluctantly proceeded with the scheme, which was opened in stages from the Aviemore end in the 1890s. For a time, shuttle services were operated to and from Aviemore, just like any Highland branch. This is an up train on the Dulnain Viaduct just outside Carr Bridge, hauled by Jones 4-4-0T No. 58 *Burghead*. (HRS collection)

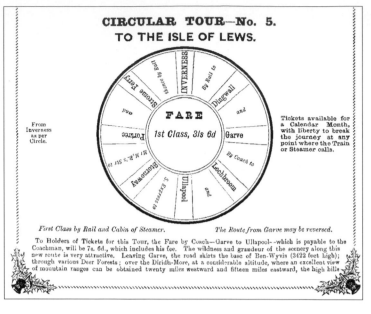

CIRCULAR TOUR—No. 5.
TO THE ISLE OF LEWS.

FARE
1st Class, 3/s 6d

From Inverness as per Circle.

Tickets available for a Calendar Month, with liberty to break the journey at any point where the Train or Steamer calls.

First Class by Rail and Cabin of Steamer.   *The Route from Garve may be reversed.*

To Holders of Tickets for this Tour, the Fare by Coach—Garve to Ullapool—which is payable to the Coachman, will be 7s. 6d., which includes his fee. The wildness and grandeur of the scenery along this new route is very attractive. Leaving Garve, the road skirts the base of Ben-Wyvis (3422 feet high); through various Deer Forests; over the Diridh-More, at a considerable altitude, where an excellent view of mountain ranges can be obtained twenty miles westward and fifteen miles eastward, the high hills

Tourists were always important to the Highland Railway so the company gradually developed facilities for them and produced publicity material. Typical was the *Programme of Arrangements* published to entice the traveller, which laid great stress on the fact that the route was 'via Dunkeld' to ensure that nobody was tempted to travel via Aberdeen and the Great North of Scotland. The 1880 version ran to twenty pages, of which two were devoted to listing fares from all parts of England and Wales. Within the Highlands, several circular tours were on offer, illustrated by listing the places within a circle. Many of the tours involved coach and steamer journeys, as shown in the example above.

An early twentieth-century innovation was a motor car set up as a mobile publicity vehicle. The headline on the other side of the vehicle reads 'The Highlands for Fishing' and advertises some of the other places served by the railway. (Courtesy of A.J. Lambert)

In Highland days, Inverness had through sleeping car services to all three London termini. This meant the Highland found itself hauling half-empty coaches over the hills from Perth. The company managed to persuade its English counterparts to reduce some of the workings to alternate days during winter. In this view of a southbound sleeper at Aviemore, headed by Cumming 4-6-0 *Clan Fraser*, four East Coast vehicles at the front, including a sleeper, and at least one West Coast vehicle are visible. (HRS collection)

Before the ferry at Strome Ferry was upgraded to take cars, there was no road from the east via Strathcarron to Kyle, so the Highland arranged to carry motor cars over that stretch of line. KS109 (an Edinburgh registration) has just been transported from Kyle to Strathcarron and shunted into the dock by Skye Bogie No. 88. (HRS collection)

For many years, the Highland produced timetable posters such as this, with the main titles highlighted in red. Various scenes from the line were included but the wording always included 'via Perth and Dunkeld' to ensure that travellers maximised their distance over Highland tracks. (HRS collection)

3

HIGHLAND TIMES

Long routes through sparsely populated country with big seasonal traffic variations required careful management. While the company never operated on a shoe string, costs were very carefully controlled and services adapted to meet demand.

Andrew Dougall came from the Perth & Dundee Railway to manage the Inverness & Nairn in 1855 and he remained as manager of the Highland until he resigned under a bit of a cloud in 1896. Dougall strongly influenced the way the railway was operated. While capital expenditure and many aspects of policy were controlled by the directors, Dougall was responsible for implementing their policy and his advice was no doubt listened to. He also controlled day-to-day expenditure and ensured that it was kept to a minimum.

After he resigned, the next two general managers both came from the North Eastern Railway (NER). Thomas Wilson, who took over in 1899, was shocked at the lax working attitudes he found. The mid-1890s was a period of financial crisis for the company, caused by the strain of developing the direct line from Aviemore. The landowners who had dominated the board gave way to men with more commercial experience, such as William Whitelaw, who later became chairman of the North British and, in turn, of the L&NER. The railway gradually returned to financial health, but the First World War proved to be another difficult period for the company because it was overloaded with traffic, particularly to serve the Grand Fleet which was stationed at Scapa Flow in the Orkneys. So the LMS inherited a line which was trying to get back on its feet.

Mixed trains operated on all lines in the early days. It was normal practice to marshal goods wagons at the front of the train, so that shunting could easily be carried out at intermediate stations. When continuous brakes became compulsory on passenger trains in 1889, the Highland objected, saying that this would lead to a reduction in passenger services. In the end, the company had to give way, but mixed formations, with the goods vehicles now behind the passenger ones, continued on some of the branch lines. This was the practice on the Dornoch branch even in BR days.

Highland train loadings varied greatly. Passenger demand was always much heavier in summer than in winter and services were planned to meet expected loads. But formations could be altered for a variety of other reasons, from the local cattle market to the Sunday school outing. The summer season produced even more problems as stock was never in the right place; the timetable included a daily down empty stock train over the main line.

This well-known photograph of a train for Strathpeffer has been published many times before, but we make no apologies for showing it again, especially as some misconceptions have grown up over the years. The Highland Railway built a palatial hotel at Strathpeffer, a spa town about 5 miles west of Dingwall, in 1911 as part of its efforts to improve tourist traffic at a time when the motor car was already affecting its first-class business. The Skye line should have run through the town, but had to avoid it because of objections from a local landowner. So a branch was opened in 1885. The Highland tried to encourage patronage of the hotel by improving services and introducing through carriages to the town. In 1914, through sleepers were operated from London King's Cross and through coaches were run on Tuesdays from both Edinburgh and Glasgow. When the hotel was opened, a train was introduced on Tuesdays which connected at Aviemore with the midday train from Perth, the main down train of the day which still ran via Forres. The Strathpeffer train ran non-stop from Aviemore to Dingwall and reached Strathpeffer at 4.15 p.m., just as the train from Perth was drawing into Inverness. The train continued to run between June and September until wartime restrictions came into force, with some variations in timing and sometimes a stop in Inverness. Why the train ran only on Tuesdays is difficult to say. It was identified as an 'Express' in some timetables, but with different names : 'Strathpeffer and Dingwall Express' one month and 'Dingwall and Strathpeffer Express' the next, so it can hardly be counted as a 'named train'. The photograph above, which appears to have been posed and therefore take for publicity use, shows it with just a destination board. The rolling stock includes a couple of lavatory bogies and one corridor coach with a six-wheel brake third at the rear, nothing special but good enough for a two-hour journey. (HRS collection)

An up train leaving Inverness headed by No. 76 *Bruce* and No. 125 *Loch Tay*. This photograph was taken before the direct line to Aviemore was built and shows a mixed rolling stock; a six-wheel straight-sided third leads in front of a collection of vans and horse boxes. The main train consists mostly of six-wheelers with a few four-wheelers and at least one bogie coach, which is likely to be a through Caledonian vehicle. (HRS collection)

A down express entering Inchmagranachan, a loop on the main line between Dunkeld and Dalguise. The tablet exchanger has been lowered, with the tablet to be dropped off in place. The train is headed by two Lochs, with No. 129 *Loch Maree* at the head. The second vehicle in the train is a West Coast Joint Stock (WCJS) 45ft family saloon. (HRS collection)

The down midday train approaching Blair Atholl behind No. 27 *Thurso Castle*, one of the second batch of Castles built by North British Locomotive Co. in 1913. The leading vehicle is one of the hybrid coaches built by the London & North Western Railway (L&NWR) for the WCJS for sleeper services where demand was not high. They contained four first-class sleeping compartments and an attendant's compartment in a full-width body and two full and one half compartments plus WC in the third-class section with a narrower body profile. (HRS collection)

Although built mainly for helping up the hill from Blair Atholl, the 0-6-4 Banking Tanks were also used on other work. No. 39 sits at Aberfeldy ready to work back to the junction at Ballinluig. Three six-wheelers are visible. The first and third vehicles are centre luggage compartment composites while in between is a brake third with wide duckets, all with flat sides. (HRS collection)

Muir of Ord is on the Far North line a few miles north of Inverness. An up train consisting of a motley collection of rolling stock arrives in 1913. The loco is a Barney 0-6-0, No. 21. Although designed mainly for goods work, these locos were all fitted with vacuum brakes and used on passenger workings. The LMS transferred some of these engines to the Glasgow area in 1938 to help with the Empire Exhibition traffic; later some found their way on to other passenger workings in that area. (HRS collection)

A lengthy up freight train standing in the Aberfeldy branch platform at Ballinluig, shunted out of the way of the main line. The locomotive is No. 127 *Loch Garry*, one of the class that was the final design by David Jones. (HRS collection)

Glenbruar on a westbound train at Achanalt, on the Kyle line, in the early 1900s. The locomotive was one of the Strath class built for the main line in 1892, but soon partly displaced by the Lochs. *Glenbruar* only worked for a short time on the Kyle line; it was maybe a bit too heavy. Achanalt was in an isolated stretch of country. The train itself consists of a mixture of six-wheeled and bogie coaches. The fourth vehicle has coupé compartments at each end. (J.L. Stevenson collection)

The Highland had its fair share of accidents, given its sparse train service. Single lines presented the greatest danger, but throughout the time that the system was operated by timetable and telegraph, no cases of mis-operation occurred. Natural disasters were harder to avoid. This is Baddengorm Burn, north of Carr Bridge on the direct line to Inverness, in 1914. Soon after noon on 18 June, a terrific thunderstorm broke out in the hills. The Baddengorm Burn, which passed under an arched railway bridge, was swollen and the arch became blocked with tree trunks and debris, undermining the bridge foundations. When the midday train from Perth reached the bridge, the damage was not apparent to the locomotive crew, but the tender derailed and the train came to a stop on the bridge. This caused the complete collapse of the arch, throwing the middle coach into the raging burn and drowning five of its passengers. This was the worst accident on the Highland. There was a similar washout about ten years later not far along the line, but that was detected in time to stop traffic. (HRS collection)

Opposite above: At Inverness the engine shed was in the form of a roundhouse. When it was opened in 1863, it contained twenty-one roads in a perfect semi-circle. It was enlarged, it is believed in 1875, by the addition of five roads at each end. Entry to the shed was through an arched doorway on each road. This became a danger as locomotives became larger, but it was not until 1949 that they were replaced by steelwork. The main entrance was through the decorative arch on the right. This well-known feature was actually a water tower. The turntable was boarded over in Highland days. It was originally 45ft and extended to 55ft 2in, as seen here. A new 63ft 2in turntable was installed in 1914, eliminating the diamond crossings on each rail. (HRS collection)

Opposite below: *Dunrobin* waits to leave Inverness on Saturday 10 September 1921, with the Duke of Sutherland's large saloon. This saloon was built by LNWR at Wolverton. Normally it was not used on journeys between Inverness and Dunrobin, but on this occasion it was waiting for the arrival of the Prince of Wales (later Edward VIII) and the Earl of Inverness, better known then as the Duke of York and later King George VI, who were going to stay at Dunrobin. (HRS collection)

Superheated Goods No. 75 on the 4.50 p.m. to Inverness after leaving Tain. This class was often used on passenger trains and became particularly associated with the Kyle line in the 1930s and '40s. The first coach is a bogie, but the rest are six-wheelers with a full brake van at the rear. (LCGB Ken Nunn collection)

South of Stanley Junction, Highland trains had running powers over the Caledonian line to Perth, where the company had a one-fifth share in the joint station, together with its own locomotive depot. The area just south of Stanley Junction was a favourite spot for H.L. Salmon, who took this photograph of the down midday train in 1922 or 1923. The first coach is a North British vehicle, which would have come over the Forth Bridge from Edinburgh. The third coach is one of the Pullman cars contracted to the Caledonian Railway. From 1922, they ran north as far as Aviemore to provide the first restaurant car facilities on the Highland. (H.L. Salmon/Stephenson Locomotive Society)

Staff from the Highland Railway were as keen as everyone else around the country to join up when the First World War broke out. Later, conscription was introduced. All this caused great problems as the railway was called on to carry far more traffic than in peacetime but without many of the skilled staff it relied on. Those who died in the conflict are recorded on the company's war memorial, which is mounted on what were originally the company's offices, to the left of the station at Inverness. It lists eighty-seven names. (Keith Fenwick)

In the First World War, as in the Second, many thousands of servicemen were carried by train to and from the Fleet in Scapa Flow. Crowded trains ran daily from London taking forces to and from postings. Refreshments were provided at Dingwall as recorded on this plaque. (Jack Kernahan)

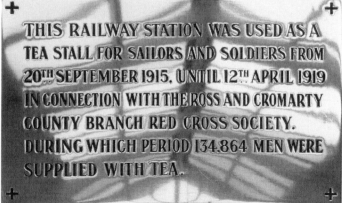

THIS RAILWAY STATION WAS USED AS A TEA STALL FOR SAILORS AND SOLDIERS FROM 20TH SEPTEMBER 1915, UNTIL 12TH APRIL 1919 IN CONNECTION WITH THE ROSS AND CROMARTY COUNTY BRANCH RED CROSS SOCIETY. DURING WHICH PERIOD 134,864 MEN WERE SUPPLIED WITH TEA.

These two views of trains climbing up from Blair Atholl to Druimuachdar in September 1932 show that the old order was still in force. In the upper photograph, a passenger train hauled by No. 14690 *Dalcross Castle* is piloted by No. 15307, one of the Banking Tanks. It was the custom for passenger trains to be piloted rather than banked. (T.D. Bell, courtesy R.K. Blencowe)

In the lower photograph, later on the same day, the final design of locomotive for the Highland Railway, Cumming's 14767 *Clan Mackinnon* built in 1921 is at the head of a freight train with an unidentified tender engine at the rear. The train itself is quite a mixture of wagons, with much use still being made of sheeted open wagons. The full brake behind the loco would have helped with braking if the vacuum was connected, as would the following vehicle. This appears to be a Midland Railway Motor Car Van; these were also used for general parcel traffic. (T.D. Bell, courtesy R.K. Blencowe)

4

LMS AND THE
SECOND WORLD WAR

The grouping of 1923 saw the Highland amalgamated into the London, Midland & Scottish Railway (LMS), along with two of the other five Scottish companies. When reorganisation of the railways was put forward just after the war, the initial proposal was that one company would be formed for Scotland. However, the companies did not support this as the new company would be inherently weaker than English ones and it would create an artificial division in the considerable Anglo-Scottish traffic. Thus the Highland found itself thrown in not only with the Caledonian and Glasgow & South Western, but also the London & North Western and the Midland. The latter two made the largest contribution to the LMS, but they were not natural bedfellows and much management effort was diverted to in-fighting over the first few years. Management in Scotland was given a bit of autonomy through a separate Scottish Local Committee of main board members. However, the LMS was a centralised organisation, unlike the L&NER, and exercised control from London, quite a long way from Dunkeld, never mind Lybster.

The Highland bequeathed a varied stock of locomotives to the new company. It had managed to partly make good the ravages of the war with the construction of sixteen modern Cumming 4-6-0s, eight each for goods and passenger duties, to add to the range of older 4-6-0s and 4-4-0s. So Highland engines carried on much as before. The works at Inverness ceased to build new stock and concentrated on repairs. A measure of independence was maintained initially, as the express passenger livery of LMS red was applied to many locomotives, which were at the most 'mixed traffic'. Still, the livery suited them well. That lasted until someone 'in authority' found out. By the late 1920s, new engines made their appearance. The Rivers, which were originally designed by the Highland but found to be overweight and were sold to the Caledonian in 1915, came north, followed by Horwich 2-6-0s, otherwise known as Crabs. But it was the arrival of Stanier's Black Five 4-6-0s in the mid-1930s that revolutionised train working and finally did away with a lot of double heading. Highland crews nicknamed them 'Hikers'. Caley engines, which came north, were also thought of in Highland terms; thus Pickersgill 4-4-0s were known as 'Caley Bens' and Jumbo 0-6-0s as 'Caley Barneys'. What the Caley drivers thought, if they ever found out, is not recorded.

Coaching stock was another matter. The Highland was generally behind other lines further south, so several vehicles were moved north to improve standards. Midland vehicles were prominent, as that line also used the vacuum brake. With several through trains to Glasgow and Edinburgh and also the overnight service to London, new LMS stock soon made its appearance.

Travel needs changed in the 1920s and '30s and this was reflected in the services provided. Several of the Highland branches were not the most convenient for passengers, who quickly took to new bus routes. A passenger in Fochabers wanting to go to Elgin, for instance, had to walk out of the village and over the river to the station to catch the train which only went as far as Orbliston, where a change was necessary. Why not jump on a bus in the middle of the village and go by the much more direct road? And it was generally cheaper! Fochabers and Burghead lost their services in 1931, Strathpeffer and Fort George struggled on into the 1940s, but with only a nominal service. Lybster also succumbed during the war. On the other hand, the more important trains were accelerated and some new services introduced in the late 1930s for the tourist traffic which was growing. Despite the recession years, holidays with pay became general and hiking grew in popularity. The Glasgow 'Fair' in particular gave the LMS operating department quite a headache. For those in employment, there was rising income and more leisure time.

The Second World War, like the First, brought an unprecedented increase in traffic. Line capacity had to be increased by bringing back passing places which had been dispensed with, new sidings had to be constructed and passenger facilities reduced.

The LMS era lasted twenty-five years. The railway continued to meet local needs and bring tourists north during the summer. Road transport took over much of the shorter distance traffic but freight held up well, given the distances involved.

Many local routes suffered from bus competition in LMS days, but some attempts were made to co-operate. Bus passengers could return by train and vice-versa, but often the rail fare was greater and a supplement had to be paid by returning bus passengers, such as this example from Inverness to Redcastle, the first station on the Fortrose branch from Muir of Ord. (Courtesy of John Roake)

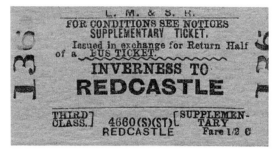

The Highland had only one class of 0-6-0 tender locomotives, known as Barneys. Twelve were built, the first in 1900. They were mostly used for goods workings on the lines north and east of Inverness, but not the main line. No. 17698 is seen here heading a goods train on the Forres line out of Inverness, while the Jinty on the right is shunting on the direct Aviemore line, 11 August 1939. (L. Hanson, courtesy David Hanson)

A southbound train sets off from Forres for the climb to Dava. This is the overnight service for London and includes coaches by both the east and west coast routes. The last three are LNER ones. The front portion includes an ex-LNWR clerestory roof sleeper. The locomotives are No. 14391 *Loch Shin* leading No. 14692 *Darnaway Castle*. (Photomatic)

Big Goods No. 17920 approaches Boat of Garten on an up goods train on 10 June 1936 with its catcher ready to drop off the tablet at the north box. By this time, the class had been relegated to lesser duties, so may have only been working as far as Aviemore. The line on the right was used by LNER trains to Craigellachie; both lines were single and diverged about 3 miles north of Boat of Garten. (Harold D. Bowtell, HRS collection)

Ex-Highland motive power continued on the Kyle line long after it was supplanted elsewhere, mainly because the turntable at Kyle could not take larger engines. It was lengthened in 1946, after which Black Fives started to appear. Here an eastbound passenger train enters Achnasheen behind Superheated Goods No. 17952 with several fish wagons at its head. These would have been vacuum fitted or, at least, through piped. (HRS collection)

There is still a strong pre-grouping flavour to this photograph of the 2.20 p.m. to Strathpeffer in the bay at Dingwall on 29 July 1926. The locomotive, Lochgorm Tank No. 16118, is in LMS black livery but the first two coaches are Highland six-wheelers, followed by one or possibly two ex-Midland clerestories. (LCGB Ken Nunn collection)

No. 14675 *Taymouth Castle* is ready to leave The Mound on an up train. LMS influence is now clear in the composition of the train. The facilities on the main line here were limited to one platform, although there was a loop to the left of the locomotive which could be used by freight trains. To the right is the branch to Dornoch with the rear of the branch train just visible. For many years, restaurant cars were swapped between down and up trains here, the branch tank doing duty as shunter. (HRS collection)

No. 14417 *Ben na Caillach* shunting at Aviemore in 1935. The photographer is standing on the island platform and looking towards the Cairngorms. The Big Bens were not an unqualified success. No. 14417 went to Aviemore in 1926 and was withdrawn ten years later. Initially it was used on the Carr Bridge line with the Inverness portion of the midday train from Perth, but latterly it was station pilot. This loco even suffered the ignominy of having its name mis-spelt as *Ben na Caillich* by the LMS. (HRS collection)

No. 14382 *Loch Moy* is seen here accelerating away from Perth station with a local train for Blair Atholl. The Highland locomotive shed was to the right and behind the train was the ticket platform on the up line. Perth was always an open station so tickets had to be collected before arrival. (HRS collection)

To meet the need for more powerful locomotives on the main line, F.G. Smith designed the River class 4-6-0s. Ordered just after the outbreak of the First World War, the first was delivered in 1915, but it was then found that the class was too heavy. This caused the resignation of Smith, although why such drastic action was necessary during the war has been the source of speculation ever since. The locomotives were sold to the Caledonian Railway but found their way back on to the Highland line in LMS days, after some fairly minimal improvements had been made to the permanent way. They powered the main expresses until the arrival of the Black Fives in the mid-1930s, after which the LMS locomotive standardisation policy led to their early demise. This was one of the final appearances of this class on the Highland, at Blair Atholl on 6 July 1939. (J.L. Stevenson)

In 1915, proposals were drawn up for two 4-4-0s to work the mail trains to the far north. It is remarkable that at this late date, such a special design was justified. With the complications of Smith's resignation, the locomotives which resulted were effectively designed by their supplier, Hawthorn Leslie. They were named *Snaigow* and *Durn*; this is the latter, by then LMS No. 14523, on a cattle train. Both locos were withdrawn in the mid-1930s. (HRS collection)

No. 14678 enters Forres in July 1945 on an afternoon train from Elgin, which is routed into the curve onto the Perth line. Pre-grouping influence can still be seen with the ex-Midland clerestory coach at the front. (J.L. Stevenson)

The railways in the Highlands, particularly north and west of Inverness, continued to play a large part in providing for the everyday transport needs long after railways elsewhere had ceased to do so. The pier at Kyle of Lochalsh was always a busy place as passengers and goods were transferred between trains and boats serving Skye and the Outer Isles. Even the sheep seemed to know where to go, as this flock finds its way towards a steamer which will take them to one of the islands for fattening. (Lens of Sutton Association)

A Stanier Black Five arrives at Inverness from the north with the fireman ready to drop off the token at Rose Street Cabin. It has just crossed the River Ness on the bridge which was swept away by floods in 1989 and is signalled to run via the Rose Street Curve to Welsh's Bridge Junction, where it will reverse into the southbound platforms. This was common practice at Inverness until well into the diesel age to provide cross platform connection to southbound trains. Similarly, the overnight train from London would run into one of the northbound platforms. The track to the right of the train is the Harbour branch. (J.L. Stevenson)

The LMS had an active policy in the management of its motive power. The Clans were displaced on the most important workings on the main line by the Rivers and several Crabs after 1928, but still had plenty of life in them. Once the first Black Fives arrived in 1934, the Clans were moved to the Oban line, where there was an urgent need for something better than the Caledonian '55' and '191' classes. In August 1939, *Clan Stewart* sets out from Oban for the climb up to Glencuitten summit. The second coach is one of the Caledonian Pullman cars which by then had been purchased by the LMS and were operated as normal dining cars. (Hamish Stevenson collection)

There was plenty of shunting to be performed at Inverness, keeping several locomotives busy. This is an ex-Caledonian 0-4-0 saddle tank, No. 16011, in about 1935, at the far end of the sidings where they join the direct line to Aviemore on the embankment. The line in the foreground was the original line to Nairn and Keith. This loco was still to be seen at Inverness in September 1958 and was withdrawn the following year. (Harold D. Bowtell, HRS collection)

In 1948, the locomotive exchanges were organised by the newly-formed British Railways to try out locomotives in different parts of the country. The Highland main line from Perth to Inverness was one of the routes chosen. No Great Western loco could take part due to clearance problems, but a Southern Railway Bulleid Pacific, *Yeovil* of the West Country class, did make the journey northwards, equipped with an LMS tender and a tablet catcher. Several runs were made in June 1948, such as with this afternoon train from Perth. (HRS collection)

Although the locomotive exchanges of 1948 attracted quite a lot of attention, particularly when the Southern Pacific ventured north to Inverness, little notice was taken of the B1 which was also tried on the route. After all, they had been working for several years out of Aberdeen on the ex-GNS lines and were to be seen occasionally in Inverness. However, No. 61292 was brought up from central Scotland and is seen here on a test train of thirteen coaches entering Aviemore. This loco, like the Pacific, was temporarily fitted with tablet-exchange apparatus. Quite a few LNER coaches are visible in the test train. (A.G. Dunbar)

5

EARLY BRITISH
RAILWAY DAYS

At nationalisation, a separate region for Scotland was set up, with its own light blue identity reflected in station signs and timetables. Alone of the six new regions, the Scottish Region was an amalgamation of two pre-nationalisation companies. LNER and LMS operating practices had to be merged, but since the former's management was less centralised, several of the senior regional posts were given to ex-LNER men. Regional power was, in any case, limited, with a 'chief officer' in charge. Many policies were decided by the Railway Executive and its master, the British Transport Commission.

As with the grouping, changes after nationalisation came slowly. Pre-war train service levels were restored gradually, interrupted by further problems such as the coal crisis of 1951. BR introduced a series of standard locomotive classes and some of these penetrated to the Highlands. Then came the modernisation plan of 1955, which envisaged the end of steam within fifteen years. In the event, the self-contained Highland area was one of the first to be completely converted, steam being virtually eliminated during 1961.

Of the branches which survived, passenger services were withdrawn from Fortrose in 1951, leaving just those to Aberfeldy and Dornoch. The latter became an enthusiasts' Mecca, as the last Highland engines, two 0-4-4Ts, operated it. But its remoteness and the restricted service of two trains each way daily made it just that bit more of a challenge. Its popularity continued when the Highland tanks were withdrawn and replaced by GWR-designed pannier tanks. All this came to an end in 1960, when the branch was closed completely along with many local stations on the Far North line.

There were individual station closures elsewhere, but with the railways nationally losing increasing amounts of money and users preferring road transport, Dr Beeching's appointment as BR chairman in 1960 heralded radical changes. Goods services to wayside stations dropped off quickly; remaining traffic was concentrated on main stations with road delivery covering larger areas. *The Reshaping of British Railways*, published in 1963, proposed to retain only the main line services from Perth and Aberdeen to Inverness. The lines north of Inverness would be closed completely, along with the Aberfeldy branch, the Dava line and many local stations. In the event, the lines north of Inverness were retained after a vociferous local campaign, but the other closures took place in 1965. This did enable further acceleration of the through services from Glasgow, Edinburgh and Aberdeen to Inverness and concentration on this longer-distance traffic, which has since grown considerably.

By 1970, the pattern of services had changed radically, but there was still a strong flavour of the old Highland. Walk onto any operational station and the buildings and signal boxes showed their ancestry. The mid-morning train from Inverness to Kyle still connected at Achnasheen with the bus service to Ullapool carrying mail, passengers and parcels, and then delivered the daily papers to Kyle of Lochalsh. The winter service on the Kyle line was still the unbalanced arrangement of three up and two down trains.

Double heading remained a feature of the Highland lines until the end of steam, particularly on the main trains between Perth and Inverness. Here, two Black Fives set off from Perth, not long before diesels took over, while a third member of the class arrives on a train from the north, 1960. (Norris Forrest/GNSRA)

By the 1930s, many of the Highland 4-4-0s were wearing out. To replace them, ex-Caledonian 4-4-0s were sent north and they continued to power many of the secondary services during the 1950s. This is a busy day at Alness. In the centre, No. 54488 is on the 3.45 p.m. Tain to Inverness train, No. 54487 is in the yard, and the rear of the 3.18 p.m. Inverness to Tain train, which is being hauled by No. 54493, can be seen on the left. (HRS collection)

Highland survivors into BR days included a Barney and a few Bens and Superheated Goods; these had all disappeared by 1954 leaving a couple of 0-4-4Ts, which were retained to work the Dornoch branch due to their light axle loading. One was withdrawn in 1956, then later that year the axle of the other broke. Here No. 55053 hauls a Dornoch-bound train near Skelbo, 23 August 1955. (J.L. Stevenson)

Balsporran was a wartime signal box about 4 miles south of Dalwhinnie. A box had been built here in Highland Railway days but was closed by the LMS. The loop had to be brought back into use to handle wartime traffic. Behind it can be seen cottages built for the signalmen and track workers. Life in these cottages, which were spread along the line, was isolated. An article in the *British Railways Scottish Region* magazine in the late 1950s notes the running of a train every other Saturday from Blair Atholl, calling at Black Tank, Dalanraoch, County March, Balsporran and Inchlea to convey workmen and families to Kingussie for provisions. That was how you got your groceries. The train was known locally as the 'Housewife's Choice', after a popular radio programme of the time. (J.L. Stevenson)

Left: To help with the collection of letters in rural areas, trains in various parts of Scotland carried post boxes, which were handed over to GPO staff at the end of the journey. This service was established in LMS days and continued until around 1960. This post box was photographed at Kyle of Lochalsh awaiting collection. (David Milton)

Right: The observation car on the turntable at Kyle of Lochalsh. This vehicle had been rebuilt in this form for the *Devon Belle* and came to the Kyle line in the late 1950s, providing an excellent view of the scenery. It was used until the mid-1960s and went to the USA in 1969 with *Flying Scotsman*, remaining there until 2007. It was then brought back and restored and in 2008 started operating on the Swanage Railway. (HRS collection)

Garve was the railhead for Ullapool, and Achnasheen served Gairloch. Branches had been proposed to both places, but the limited traffic never justified construction. Connection by specially designed buses able to carry passengers, parcels and mail continued into the 1970s. This 1965 bus provides convenient connection to an eastbound train at Achnasheen in 1972, not long before direct road services to and from Inverness led to the loss of this traffic by rail. (Norris Forrest/GNSRA)

Pullman cars were introduced on the Caledonian Railway just before the First World War to provide restaurant and buffet facilities. The LMS took over the distinctively designed vehicles in 1933 and several passed to British Railways ownership. One was a regular feature of the morning train from Inverness to Wick, but it only ran as far as The Mound, where it was transferred to the southbound train. The branch tank was used to do the necessary shunting, as seen here on 7 October 1953. (J.L. Stevenson)

Achnasheen usually saw only three or four trains each way daily, but long periods of inactivity could be broken when trains crossed. This was particularly the case at about midday when the morning passenger trains crossed and, as with the Wick trains, exchanged the restaurant car. Unlike The Mound, there was no shunter here so the train engine had to take the car from the rear of the Kyle-bound train and add it onto the front of the Inverness-bound one. In some years the westbound freight was also in the station at the same time. This view from the footbridge looks east, with the restaurant car about to be added to the front of the train from Kyle. (Hugh Davies/Photos from the Fifties)

Banking continued on the climb to Druimuachdar until the end of steam days, with LMS 2-6-4Ts usually performing these duties. Here No. 42169 buffers up to the rear of a passenger train at Blair Atholl prior to the slog up to Dalnaspidal. (HRS collection)

In March 1961, D6151 and D5123 head the 9.40 a.m. from Inverness to Aviemore via Forres, conveying through coaches to both Edinburgh and Glasgow. D6121 was a North British type 2, one of the classic failures of the BR modernisation plan; they could not be trusted to work on their own. Later they were used north of Aberdeen and carefully looked after by Inverurie Works. Some were re-engined, but even those did not last long into the 1970s. (Norris Forrest/GNSRA)

The Aberfeldy branch was the first to be built and the last to close, on 3 May 1965. Caledonian 0-4-4Ts were the motive power for many years after suitable ex-Highland engines had been withdrawn. Here, No. 55218, in grubby condition, waits to leave Ballinluig for Aberfeldy. Normally formed of just one coach, through coaches were operated daily to and from Perth, returning on the 4 p.m. train. BR 2-6-4Ts took over from the Caley engines in 1960-1, followed by type 2 diesels shortly afterwards. (Author's collection)

In January 1965, D5336 gets its tank filled at Aberfeldy from a hose which clearly let out as much water as it delivered to the loco. The coach was an LNER Thompson design; this vehicle has been preserved by the SRPS. (Norris Forrest/GNSRA)

The modernisation plan of 1955 recognised the need for cheap, lightweight trains for branch lines. The result was the four-wheeled railbus. Initially brought north to work the ex-GNS Speyside line, they were also used on Aviemore to Inverness local runs. SC79969 is sitting in the centre road at Inverness between turns of duty in June 1962. Not only were they unreliable but the ride was at best uncomfortable. (HRS collection)

A Brush type 3, later class 31, No. D5511 approaches Millburn Junction, Inverness, on the direct line from Aviemore in June 1958 on a test run, believed to be the first time a main line diesel reached Inverness. Diesels were to become a common sight two years later, but class 31s were never used in Scotland. The track in the foreground is the original line to Nairn; the newer line crossed over it just east of Millburn Junction. (Sandy Edward/GNSRA)

6

PROVIDING FOR MODERN NEEDS

The early 1970s saw the growth of the North Sea oil industry, bringing hope of much greater traffic to the railways in the Highlands and economic prosperity generally. Expected demand for sea-platforms resulted in several construction yards being set up, including one at Loch Kishorn on the west coast, but it is has been the growth of support services, particularly around Inverness, that has had the greatest impact on travel demand.

While freight trains continued to run during the 1970s, by the mid-1980s there was little general traffic left. Some specialist flows, such as cement to Inverness, prospered; others, such as timber, have come and gone according to market needs. Privatisation has, however, led to a resurgence in freight.

Meanwhile passenger traffic has grown steadily, but with continuing financial pressures the search for economies has been relentless. In the late 1980s, new diesel multiple units took over most of the passenger workings on all lines. Lighter trains with better acceleration meant less track maintenance costs and faster journey times. The labour-intensive signalling system north of Inverness was swept away in 1986 when the Radio Tokenless Block was introduced. Despite some operating problems, this enabled all station staff to be withdrawn except at Dingwall, Wick, Thurso and Kyle. At the same time, it became economical to operate Sunday services. The Scottish Region was transformed into ScotRail under the energetic leadership of Chris Green.

When privatisation came, passenger operation was taken over by the National Express group for the first franchise period and then, in 2004, by First Group, operating as First ScotRail. Scottish services continue to depend on a considerable financial subsidy, particularly in the Far North, so much of the service provision is influenced by the Scottish Executive and its administrative arm, Transport for Scotland.

Over the last forty years, the remains of the Burghead and Inverness harbour branches have closed, but otherwise the network has remained the same and several stations have reopened.

Until 1970, road travel between Dingwall and Kyle of Lochalsh involved crossing Loch Carron by the Strome Ferry. The railway ran on the south side of the loch, so it was decided to build a single-track road alongside it to cut out the ferry crossing. At the narrowest stretch, the hillside was cut back and the railway moved to a new embankment to make room for the road. An avalanche shelter had to be constructed  to protect both the railway and the road. This can be seen under construction in this view from a westbound train in 1970. Stabilisation work has also been needed several times after rockfalls, and a section of railway has had to be rebuilt further out onto the loch. There has even been talk of replacing the road by a bridge at Strome Ferry. (Keith Fenwick)

Among the projects set up by the government to support the North Sea oil industry was a fabrication plant at Loch Kishorn. Transport was a problem, so the pier at Strome Ferry was rebuilt and new sidings laid; they can be seen under construction in this photograph from 1974. In the event the yard produced very little and the sidings and pier soon fell into disuse. But this project did have one positive benefit. With completion of the road along Loch Carron in prospect, closure of the Kyle line was scheduled to take effect in 1974 once all the roadworks had been completed, but by 1974, it was clear that the line had to be retained and the closure was never implemented. (Keith Fenwick)

Motorail services carrying cars and their passengers became popular in the 1950s. It was far more comfortable starting a family holiday without a long drive in pre-motorway days. In June 1973, class 50 No. 413 is assembling a morning service from Inverness to York. The cars were loaded on platform 1 just out of view on the left, but these had already been shunted to platform 2. The coaches are about to be added on to the front of the train. This service ran overnight on most days, hence the inclusion of sleepers. Motorail services faded away in the 1980s as the road network improved and stock and locomotives for such special workings became harder to find. (Keith Fenwick)

Passengers are getting off this train at platform 2 at Inverness in 1979 because it has come from Wick and Thurso and has run past the station on the Rose Street Curve, then reversed into the platform to provide easy connection with southbound trains. Although this practice ceased a few years ago, one train is still run regularly via the Rose Street Curve to avoid closure procedures having to be instituted. The locomotive is No. 26018. (HRS collection)

Two type 2 diesels, showing that they too could emit clouds of dark smoke, taking the 'Royal Highlander' northwards out of Aviemore in October 1974 with a generous provision of mark I sleepers, a design introduced by BR in 1957. Some sleeper services loaded so well, particularly the up Sunday train, that triple heading was needed. (Keith Fenwick)

A northbound freight at Helmsdale in July 1969 hauled by D5118, later class 24. Despite the closure of many wayside stations to goods service, a variety of traffic was still handled. (Keith Fenwick)

Class 47s became common on the Perth line in the 1970s and on the Aberdeen line a few years later. At last, double heading could be avoided. A northbound sleeper enters Aviemore in June 1975. In those days, the train carried English newspapers north to Inverness; they could be purchased at the station bookstall within ten minutes of the train arriving. Connecting trains carried them forward, so it was the middle of the afternoon before they could be purchased in Kyle of Lochalsh. Glasgow and Edinburgh newspapers also came by train, but reached Inverness around 6 a.m. (Keith Fenwick)

With the run-down of services in the mid-1960s, it was decided that several passing places and the double track section on the main line were no longer required. However, a new passing loop was constructed at Dalanraoch, halfway up the northbound climb to Druimuachdar. This view was taken from the north end looking south in April 1973, by which time work to redouble the section from Blair Atholl to Dalwhinnie was in progress. (J.L. Stevenson)

Improvements have been made to many stations over the years to bring them up to modern standards, with new lighting, proper platform surfaces and shelters for waiting passengers. This is Garve, from the rear of an eastbound train in 1992, where the platforms have been raised to coach door level. The gap between the tracks was wider in the loops on the Kyle line as there was a proposal when the line was being built to carry fishing boats by rail between Strome and Dingwall to avoid the long passage round the north of Scotland. Cranes were ordered from Cowan, Sheldon in Carlisle, but the scheme was put on hold when money ran out in 1870 and never revived. (Keith Fenwick)

The Highland lines became popular with excursions in the 1970s. Initially run mainly for enthusiasts, they soon proved attractive to the general public who wanted a day out in wonderful scenery. Then came weekend trips from further afield which later turned into luxury trains including sleepers. This is the Wirral Railway Circle's *Great Britain* passing through Dunrobin on the way from Penzance to Wick and Thurso. Dunrobin Castle, the Duke of Sutherland's seat, was a short walk away to the left. (Norris Forrest/GNSRA)

Class 37s took over from type 2s north and east of Inverness around 1980 and were the staple motive power until modern multiple units arrived in the late 1980s. They proved to be reliable machines, hardly stretched by the loads hauled, but their six-wheeled bogies cannot have been gentle on the track. Some are still in use as they approach their fiftieth birthday. Gradually mark II

carriages also appeared as the mark Is wore out. After the first tranche of diesel units arrived, locomotive-hauled trains continued on the Kyle line during the summer months. In 1992, 37088 in blue livery waits with a morning train for Kyle composed of mark IIa coaches painted green and white. (Keith Fenwick)

To encourage tourists, the trailer car from a first-generation diesel unit was converted to an observation car named *Hebridean*. It is seen here at Inverness in June 1992. Swivel seats were provided. A supplement was charged for travel in the vehicle, in which a commentary was given and refreshments were available. This recalls the ex-*Devon Belle* observation car run to Kyle from the late 1950s until the mid-1960s. In those days, it was possible to turn the car at Kyle so that it was on the rear of the train for the return journey, but *Hebridean* had to remain at the east end of the train, behind the locomotive. A supplement was still charged! (Keith Fenwick, upper, Forbes Munro, lower)

A typical main line train in the years before class 158s arrived is illustrated by this up train at Dalwhinnie in June 1992. Class 47 No. 595 *Confederation of British Industry* is in Inter-City livery and hauls a rake of early mark II coaches in the original ScotRail livery of dark blue upper panels and white below, with a light blue band. (Keith Fenwick)

When diesel multiple units took over north of Inverness in the late 1980s, class 156s were first on the scene and provided good views, although the seats were not the most comfortable for a long journey. Here, a return working from Kyle is seen near Plockton. (A.G. Murdoch/ GNSRA)

Sleeper service popularity declined nationally in the 1990s so much that complete withdrawal was in prospect. However, they survived with some restructuring and now bring First ScotRail services to London. Inverness is served by a train which also carries portions for Aberdeen and Fort William and is divided at Edinburgh. Inverness also has an important part to play as it services all ScotRail sleepers. Stock is rotated on an eight-day basis, so that every coach regularly reaches the town. As First ScotRail's only locomotive-hauled train, motive power is provided by EWS, usually a class 67 north of Edinburgh. The northbound train is seen here near Moy, 28 February 2005. (Mark G. Lyons)

In the early hours of 7 February 1989, the River Ness was in full flood and washed away the Victoria Viaduct at Inverness, isolating all the lines to the north. Fortunately, this was discovered in time to stop the first train. The railway quickly rose to the challenge and organised services from Dingwall to Kyle and the far north. Bus connections were provided between Dingwall and Inverness. A maintenance depot was needed and this was built at Muir of Ord, where land was readily available. The building is seen here under construction, April 1989. (J.L. Stevenson)

The permanent way on the Highland main line proved inadequate to take the River class 4-6-0s when they were delivered in 1915, but the standard has been gradually improved over the years. Long-welded rail and deep ballast have been provided over the last thirty years to cope with higher speed passenger trains and heavy goods wagons. By contrast, maintenance on the lines north of Inverness has been tuned to the operation of diesel multiple units. Sleeper replacement has been limited and rail life extended, enabling considerable economy to be achieved. However, larger steam engines can now operate to Inverness. Scottish-based A4 Pacific *Union of South Africa* has paid several visits in recent years, hauling special trains such as the return leg of the *Great Britain* railtour near Ralia, south of Newtonmore, on 14 April 2007. The second locomotive is K4 *The Great Marquis*. (Chris Boyd)

Opposite below: After privatisation, class 170 three-car multiple units were introduced and gradually took over many workings on the main line from Perth. One of these units enters Blair Atholl on a down train in July 2001. The *Royal Scotsman* luxury tour train is in the up platform. (Mark G. Lyons)

Right: A class 67 waits in the up platform at Blair Atholl in September 2006. The photograph was taken from the level crossing. The metal grid in the foreground carries the Train Protection and Warning System (TPWS) transmitter. This system was introduced nationally to ensure that drivers do not pass signals at danger. However, on the lines north and west of Inverness, where radio tokenless block is in force, trains have to run into crossing loops more slowly and about twenty minutes had to be added to the journey time between Inverness and Wick. (Howard Geddes)

From right to left: a class 170, class 158 and the coaches of the London sleeper, all in National Express's ScotRail livery, at Inverness in 2003. (Keith Fenwick)

Just north of Inverness, the line crosses the Caledonian Canal as it joins the Beauly Firth. The swing bridge over the canal, which can be seen on the right, is operated by the signaller, his box being just out of view on the left. (Keith Fenwick)

A view looking north, showing the bridge to the canal closed. The bridge is locked in place before the signals can be cleared. Originally, it was hand operated, but power operation was introduced many years ago. (Keith Fenwick)

7

HIGHLAND LOCOMOTIVES AND ROLLING STOCK

The Inverness & Nairn was a short, easily graded line for which 2-2-2s with 6ft driving wheels were adequate. Four such engines of the Raigmore class were obtained, followed when the line to Keith opened by seven 2-4-0s with 5ft driving wheels of the Seafield class. Similar engines were ordered for the extension north of Inverness. When the line to Perth was under construction, locomotive requirements seem to have been given little thought, as yet more 2-2-2s for passenger trains, the Glenbarry class, and 2-4-0s for goods work, were ordered, both with some improvements to those already in service. A further batch of 2-4-0s was delivered in 1864.

For several years, further investment was limited to purchasing a couple of tank engines. William Stroudley, who became locomotive superintendent in 1865, was unable to make his mark before he departed to the London, Brighton & South Coast Railway (LB&SCR) in 1870. It was not until the line to Wick and Thurso was nearing completion that the first 4-4-0s were ordered, the Duke class. This set the pattern for several designs of 4-4-0s by David Jones, who took over from Stroudley and remained in charge until 1896. Outside cylinders, Allan straight link motion and Crewe-type front end were to be seen in the Duke, Clyde Bogie, Strath and Loch classes, as well as the Skye Bogie, a smaller version designed for that line. Then, in 1894, Jones introduced his last design, the Big Goods. Intended specifically for the goods trains over the main line, these were the first 4-6-0s in the British Isles; the first of the class, No. 103, has been preserved.

Peter Drummond took over in 1896 and produced a wider variety of types: the Highland's only 0-6-0s, a 4-6-0 for passenger working, two classes of 4-4-0s and tank engine designs for branch work, shunting and banking. His successor was F.G. Smith, whose only design was the 4-6-0 River class. When the first of the class arrived, it was found that it was too heavy and Smith was forced to resign; a strange affair, which may have had as much to do with poor availability of the locomotive fleet as the deficiencies of this new design. Cumming, his successor, built two large 4-6-0 classes for passenger and goods work, and a couple of modern 4-4-0s for the Far North line. Thus the Highland went out with, on one hand, some elderly 4-4-0s ready for withdrawal and, on the other, several very modern 4-6-0s which out-lasted the LMS.

The late 1920s saw the return of the Rivers after some improvements to the bridges and in the early 1930s, LMS 5P5F 2-6-0s, commonly known as Crabs, came north for the main line. The first of Stanier's Black Fives ran on the Highland lines in August 1934 and by the following year there were sufficient of them to take over most of the main line duties. These were the mainstay until dieselisation, although some BR standard class 5s appeared and several Caley 4-4-0s came north to replace worn out Highland engines on lighter duties. Both LMS- and BR-designed class 4 2-6-4Ts also appeared. BR did consider allocating Clan Pacifics to the main line, but that plan was dropped.

Dieselisation came early to the Highlands, virtually eliminating steam by 1961. Diesel multiple units were introduced on the Aberdeen to Inverness run, at last giving that line a proper through service, and units also worked local services at the southern end of the main line. Otherwise it was mainly a case of replacing steam locos with type 2 diesels (mainly what were later classes 25 and 27), with a few type 1s (later class 20) for freight work. During the 1970s, type 4s, of classes 40, 47 and 50, were in regular use. Workings north of Inverness were largely taken over by class 37s in the 1980s, by which time classes 40 and 50 had disappeared from the area.

The Sprinter revolution eliminated most locomotive-hauled passenger trains in the late 1980s. Class 156s were used initially north of Inverness and to Aberdeen, later replaced by class 158s which, after a recent refurbishment, look set to operate services for many years to come. South of Inverness, class 158s have generally given way to class 170s.

Thus today, multiple units form nearly all the regular services. The only exceptions are the daily HST to London and the overnight sleeper (usually class 67 hauled). The remaining freight is hauled by class 66s. The regular tourist workings, which are still a feature, are usually hauled by class 37s, but these are now nearing the end of their working lives.

No. 9 *Aldourie* appeared in 1871 as a nominal rebuild of a Raigmore class 2-2-2 of 1855, but this was really an 'accountant's' rebuilding as there was very little of the original locomotive left. (HRS collection)

No. 7 *Fife* started life as a Seafield class 2-4-0, built for goods work on the Inverness & Aberdeen Junction Railway (I&AJ) by Hawthorns & Co. of Leith and delivered in 1858. It was rebuilt as a 4-4-0 for working on the Kyle line in 1875, following the rebuilding two years earlier of another of the same class. 4-4-0s were more suitable than 2-4-0s on that curving route. *Fife* lasted until 1899, its last duties being as a shunter at Forres. (HRS collection)

Stroudley was only able to produce one new design while at Inverness, an 0-6-0 shunting tank known as the Lochgorm Tank class. One was put in service in 1869, followed by two more after Stroudley left. No. 57 dates from 1872; it was rebuilt in 1897 and withdrawn as 16119 in December 1932. Clearly Stroudley developed this design into his well-known Terriers on the LB&SCR. Five of those actually came north to the Highland during the First World War so the two classes must have worked alongside each other. (Author's collection)

No. 65 *Dalraddy* was one of the Dukes, the first of Jones' 4-4-0 classes. Introduced in 1874, they immediately took over the main trains on the Perth line, where they proved their reliability and power and remained the principle class until the arrival of the Clyde bogies in 1886. Later, some of the Dukes moved to the Far North and Kyle lines and others were relegated to piloting duties. Withdrawal took place between 1907 and 1923. (HRS collection)

The Duke of Sutherland's engine *Dunrobin* at Helmsdale in March 1950, stored beside No. 14409 *Ben Alisky* which was withdrawn that month. At the formation of BR, the Duke's right to run his locomotive to and from Inverness was extinguished and the locomotive was stored for some time before being purchased by the Lincolnshire Trading Co., which arranged to house it at New Romney on the Romney, Hythe & Dymchurch Railway. Later that month, the loco ran south under its own steam with the small saloon in tow. (A.G. Murdoch/GNSRA)

The celebrated Big Goods was David Jones' answer to powering goods trains over the main line, replacing elderly 2-4-0s. Fifteen were built in 1894 in one batch and were a success from the start. They continued on the main line until the arrival of the Rivers in 1928 and then gravitated to lighter duties. The last was withdrawn in 1940, but No. 103 was put aside for preservation in 1934. In 1958, it was returned to running order and most of the original features restored. Here it is seen at Nairn in 1965 working one of the specials run to celebrate the centenary of the formation of the Highland Railway. Later that year it was withdrawn and subsequently put on display in the Glasgow Museum of Transport. (Norris Forrest/GNSRA)

No. 140 *Taymouth Castle* sitting on the turntable in the roundhouse at Inverness in Highland days. The Castle class was designed by Peter Drummond and introduced in 1900, providing the mainstay of main line power until after the First World War. Six appeared in 1900, four in 1902, then seven between 1910 and 1913. Finally, another three with larger wheels appeared in 1917. (HRS collection)

Such was the success of the design of the Castles that, when the North British Locomotive Co. secured an order for fifty medium-power locomotives for the French State Railways in 1911, it simply adapted the Castle design. Delivery of all fifty was completed during the summer of that year, the order having been placed in January. This is Chemin de Fer de l'Etat No. 230–330. All were withdrawn by 1938, but one or two were seen intact by observant members of the British Expeditionary Force in 1939–40. (J.L. Stevenson)

The Small Ben class was Drummond's first design, intended for faster and lighter work on the North and East lines. With a longer and higher boiler than the Lochs, inside cylinders and built-up chimney without louvres, it was quite a change, but much more in keeping with contemporary practice. Twenty engines were built to this design between 1898 and 1906. They continued to work around the system until BR days, many receiving replacement Caledonian-designed boilers. The last survivor, *Ben Alder*, was earmarked for preservation and lingered around until the early 1960s when, without any attempt to get outside help, it was scrapped as there was no chance of funding restoration. (HRS collection)

As well as the Crabs and Black Fives introduced by the LMS, several other locomotive types were moved about the system. Glasgow & South Western Railway (G&SWR) 0-6-2Ts, similar to the Highland's 0-6-4T Banking Tanks, came north; both were Peter Drummond's designs. Several Caledonian types were also transferred. Pickersgill 4-4-0s were the mainstay of lesser services in the 1950s. There were also several tank engines, such as Caledonian 0-6-0Ts for shunting. Caley 0-4-4Ts worked the Aberfeldy branch until 1961 and as shunters elsewhere. Above is a rarer beast, an 0-4-2T built originally for use on the Killin branch. It saw out its days in the late 1940s shunting at Inverness, including the harbour line. (HRS Collection)

The Rivers looked impressive machines, especially from this angle. This is LMS No. 14756, the first of the class, which started life as HR No. 70 *River Ness*. Said to be heavy on coal, they were otherwise modern and capable. With a little modification to the permanent way and a better understanding of track stresses, the LMS put them to work on the Highland main line in 1927. After 1934 they were replaced by Black Fives. Such a numerically small class of six was not going to last long under LMS standardisation; only the war kept the last two going, double heading sixteen-coach troop trains between Ayr and Girvan. (R.G. Jarvis)

Cumming Clan class 4-6-0s of 1919 was the last to be introduced by the Highland and soon proved its worth on the main line. Although, good at uphill work and fast downhill, they did not do so well on level track. Clans worked the principal turns until the arrival of the Crabs around 1930, but there was still plenty of work to keep them going in the summer and the Crabs could not work on the Dava line. With the arrival of the Black Fives, the whole class gravitated to the Oban line, which was sorely in need of something to handle increased train loads, by 1935. Black Fives replaced them in turn by 1939, so the Clans went back to the Highland, working their last years mainly north of Inverness. The last was withdrawn in 1950. This is No. 14766, *Clan Chattan*, originally No. 54. (HRS collection)

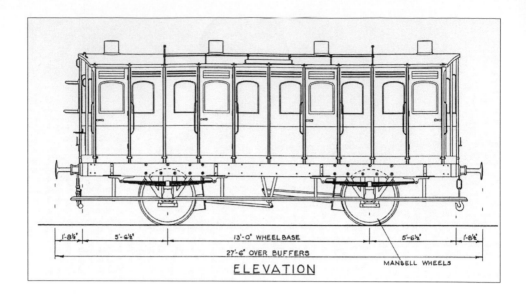

1'-8½" 5'-6½" 13'-0" WHEEL BASE 5'-6½" 1'-8½"

27'-6" OVER BUFFERS

MANSELL WHEELS

ELEVATION

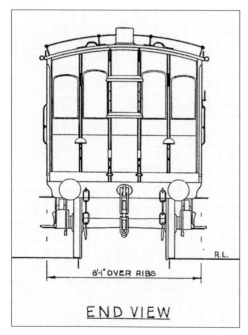

R.L.

8'-1" OVER RIBS

END VIEW

Early Highland coaches were four-wheelers, purchased from leading builders of the day such as Brown & Marshall and Metropolitan Carriage & Wagon Co. It was not long, however, before the Highland developed its own design characteristics. Initially, this was in the form of ribbed sides and curved ends. This is illustrated in the drawing (above and left, by Peter Tatlow) of an I&AJ first of *c.* 1863. Rib sides lasted for some years, refined by Jones (as illustrated lower opposite). First-class coupé ends continued and were favoured for most of the nineteenth century. Eventually the rib sides gave way to more conventional panelling. Later developments into bogie coaches with lavatories and corridors followed what happened nationally but usually with some delay; the Highland was always conscious of the additional cost so introduced these improvements to through vehicles to the south first.

From 1906, vertical matchboarding was used for body sides and this practice continued until the grouping. By that time, construction of vehicles had ceased altogether at Inverness, and outside contractors, usually Hurst Nelson or R&Y Pickering, were used. Quite a variety of coach configurations appeared, ranging from simple non-corridor firsts and thirds to composites, saloons and combination sleepers and third compartment vehicles for the overnight services.

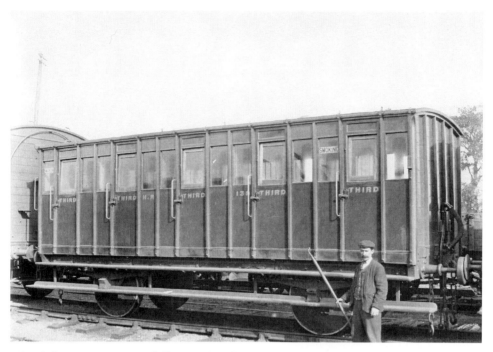

Rib-sided construction is well illustrated in this early five-compartment third. The photograph was taken much later in the life of the vehicle, after vacuum brakes had been fitted. (HRS collection)

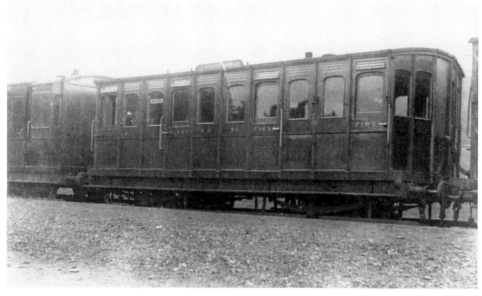

Jones carried on with rib sides and coupé ends but in a more refined style, typified by this first class coach at Aberfeldy. This contained two full and two coupé compartments, the coupés at the curved ends affording a better view of the passing scenery. However, if a compartment was immediately behind a locomotive, it was locked out of use. (HRS collection)

Jones evolved an even more complex end design, with a distinctive boot which was said to be needed to improve the restricted legroom of the outer seats. Anyone attempting to model the shape is presented with a considerable challenge if starting from flat metal. After withdrawal, this coach body found a home in an Inverness garden. (J.L. Stevenson)

By 1890, when this six-wheeled third was built, construction was more conventional, with panelled sides. Livery was dark olive green, but in the mid-1890s several railways adopted brighter liveries. So the Highland painted the upper panels white from 1897 and this continued until 1902, when economies forced a return to overall green. After 1912, coaches were painted moss green. (HRS collection)

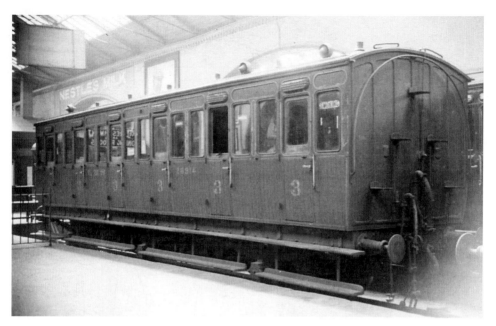

Drummond's first design was a six-wheeled six-compartment third. This one, LMS No. 26914, started life as Third No. 61 in 1897 and was photographed at Inverness in June 1938. The design must have been well liked, as further batches were built in 1907 and 1909. (HRS/ Hunter collection)

The Highland was not quick to adopt bogie coaches, but did so in 1896 for through workings to Glasgow and Edinburgh. Bogie coaches came in a variety of forms, those for through workings having lavatories. Various permutations of internal lavatories were tried, some providing facilities to selected compartments only, before a full internal corridor was adopted. Above is a lavatory third built by Hurst Nelson in 1904 with seven compartments, four of which had a lavatory each and the other three no such facilities. This photograph was taken at Inverness in August 1948. (J.L. Stevenson)

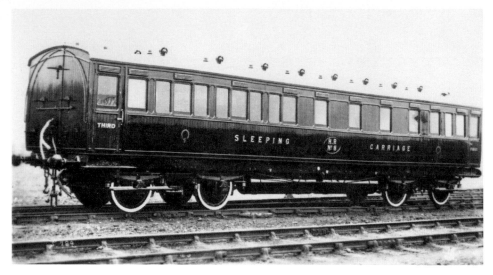

The Highland introduced its first sleeping cars in 1880, running on the overnight trains between Perth and Inverness and also Inverness and Wick. A couple of Pullmans were obtained for this duty but by 1905 patronage had dropped. To replace them and allow through running to Glasgow, two new vehicles with four sleeping compartments and three ordinary third class ones, one a coupé, were obtained from Hurst Nelson. Vertical matchboarding was used below the waist and these coaches were varnished instead of being painted. (HRS collection)

This detail of a diagram 36 bogie third shows the vertical matchboarding which was favoured by the Highland. Several Highland bogie vehicles survived into the 1950s and managed to travel far and wide. One was even photographed on the Lickey incline in 1954. (HRS Orbach collection)

Mail had always been an important traffic on the Highland. The GPO paid well and provided a guaranteed income. It caused the running of Sunday trains until Sunday deliveries ceased just after the First World War. With the long run up the main line, the GPO required the provision of sorting vans and the use of exchange apparatus at smaller stations to ensure the best overall journey time. The Highland built several GPO Sorting Vans. This is LMS 30322, built as Highland No. 6 in 1916 and the final design. It continued in use until 1961, when it was replaced by a BR standard design, operating between Perth and Inverness then further north to Dingwall and Helmsdale. This view was taken at St Rollox, Glasgow, in March 1949 when it was still in LMS livery. (J.L. Stevenson)

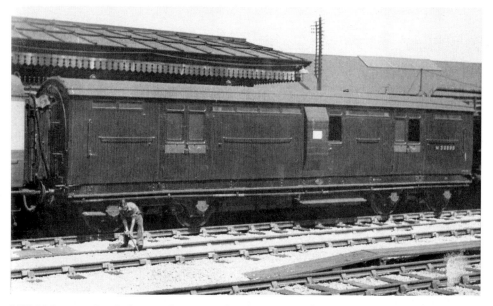

M32898 was a Smith design of Bogie Brake, diagram 51, built by R&Y Pickering in 1917. It was on its travels when photographed at Gloucester in June 1949. (G.S.L. Lloyd/HRS collection)

After the grouping, there was an urgent need for newer coaches and the LMS drafted in vehicles from various other pre-grouping companies. Dining car services were also introduced on all the main routes. Dining cars from the L&NWR, Lancashire and Yorkshire (L&Y), Midland and G&SWR were to be seen north of Perth, as well as the Pullman cars which the Caledonian had contracted and started operating to Aviemore in 1922. Above is ex-G&SWR dining car No. 3, which survived into BR days. (HRS Orbach collection)

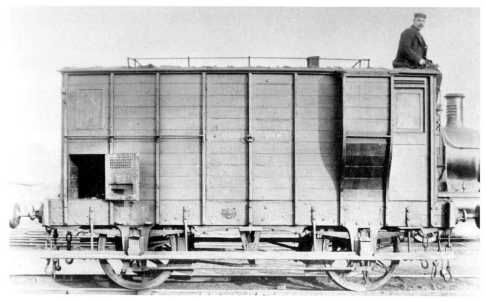

This photograph of an early goods brake van is believed to have been specially posed with the railwayman sitting atop to illustrate how a guard may have travelled in early days, even though there is a ducket on the side. The dog box door, bottom left, has also been left in the open position. This gave access to a transverse compartment the height and width of the door. Dog boxes were a common feature of passenger brake vans. (HRS collection)

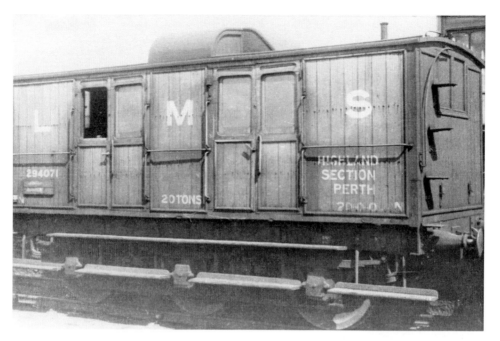

Highland wagons were very similar to those on other lines but the steep gradients called for a beefier brake van. This 20-ton six-wheeled example is typical of the ones built in the twentieth century. The guard's lookout was omitted from later examples. (HRS collection)

Much coal to the Highlands was carried by sea. Locomotive coal originally came that way, but later rail transport was used throughout. This example was one of a batch of fifty obtained from R.Y. Pickering & Co. at £77 each in 1914. (HRS collection)

The transport of sheep and cattle was always important. Large numbers of sheep had to be moved each year between summer and winter grazing, often many miles. It was worthwhile therefore to build dedicated double-deck sheep wagons, such as the example above. Of course, extra cleaning was needed after each use, especially on the lower deck. There were also specifically-designed open wagons which were fitted with removable wooden pens, or 'flakes', for sheep traffic. (HRS collection)

Meat wagons, such as this example built by R.Y. Pickering & Co. in 1911, were fitted for operation in passenger trains. (HRS collection)

8

STATION BUILDINGS

Highland Railway stations were a mixed bunch. Some were substantial stone buildings with generous provision for both passengers and staff, others little more than timber huts. When the first lines were opened, only temporary arrangements were ready. The company did not know how successful some of the stations would be, so delayed building permanent structures. Many buildings date from the first few years after opening.

A few themes can be detected in the design of buildings, although just about every station was different. The I&AJ favoured two-storey stone buildings incorporating living accommodation for the stationmaster; similar buildings were built on the line north from Inverness as far as Bonar Bridge in a contemporary Italianate style. Three of the stations on the Kyle line had large double-gabled buildings with upstairs living accommodation. Blair Atholl had a substantial building in stone with elaborate ornamentation in recognition of the Duke of Atholl, who had his own waiting room in the east wing and a viewing balcony on the road side of the building.

Several important stations were rebuilt and enlarged during the 1880s, long buildings with a multitude of rooms for different uses were constructed, but included no living accommodation; the stationmaster justified a separate house at these places. Fashion was followed in the 1890s when wooden buildings were constructed, but again these were of generous proportions and did not include living accommodation. The termini at Wick and Thurso had large sheds under which the platform ran to provide shelter for the passengers and covered storage for coaches. Overall roofs also featured at the original terminal stations at Dunkeld and Strome Ferry, as well as at the GNSR-owned Keith Junction.

Smaller stations had to make do with much more modest structures, some in stone, others wooden. Most were plain without any of the ornamentation which featured on the larger buildings.

The Highland constructed platform awnings at only a few places: Aviemore, Kingussie, Grantown, Strathpeffer and Dingwall. Some others had an open-fronted area under the main roof, with support columns along the front.

At nearly all stations with crossing loops, the 'opposite' platform had to make do with a simple shelter, usually without any heating, with a central door and windows on either side.

Orbliston station building was erected by the I&AJ in 1859, a year after the station was opened. The stationmaster's accommodation was at the far end. When photographed here in 1991 it was derelict but it has since been renovated as a private house. (Keith Fenwick)

The three original passing places on the Kyle line, at Garve, Achnasheen and Strathcarron, had similar substantial stone buildings. Achnasheen is seen here in the 1970s. The original stone has been rendered. The building to the right was the hotel which burnt down in 1995. This station building was converted into a bunkhouse in the 1990s and Strathcarron and Garve are now in residential use, with protective walls in front of them. (Jack Kernahan)

Most stations on the far north line were of plain design and fitted in well with the countryside. This is Forsinard, where the line left the road to Melvich on the north coast and headed north eastwards towards Georgemas Junction. The station building has now found a new use as a visitor centre run by the RSPB for the Forsinard Flows nature reserve. (Norris Forrest/Great North of Scotland Railway Association)

Thurso and Wick stations were similar stone buildings supporting a large overall roof which covered a short length of the platform and run-round loop. The booking and other offices were in the gable on the right. This is Thurso in 1988. (Simon de Souza)

Thurso roof was supported on wooden trussing and part of the roof was glazed to give some illumination inside. Even so, these sheds were dark places in steam days. This photograph was taken on 23 June 2003 and shows Deltic 55009 on a special; a second Deltic at the other end enabled the train to reverse easily at Wick, Georgemas and Thurso. (Mark G. Lyons)

The building at Golspie was in a distinctive style, no doubt to impress the Duke of Sutherland and his guests. It was designed by William Fowler and built in 1868. This is the view from the approach road in May 1973 with the site of the goods yard on the left. The end of the platform verandah can be seen on the right. After several years out of use, the building, which is grade B listed, has been sympathetically converted for residential use. Some of the features here are also to be seen in the building at Helmsdale. (Keith Fenwick)

This is the exterior of Dingwall station, one of those rebuilt in the 1880s, as seen by someone approaching from the town. The main entrance is by the side door under the small gable near the centre of the building. The booking office was to its right. In one of the gardens on the left there was a Highland coach. (Author's collection)

Above: Pitlochry was another 1880s rebuild. This is one of the few stations which is still staffed and, with the added benefit of an active local support group, is kept in very good order. It is seen here in 1991. (Keith Fenwick)

Right: One very interesting aspect of these buildings are the stone finials on the gable ends. All are different carvings – rose, thistle, fleur-de-lys (or Prince of Wales feathers), star and recumbent half moon. The rose at Pitlochry is seen here. (Keith Fenwick)

Below: The downside building at Pitlochry is a substantial wooden shelter. That at Nairn, below, is to the same design and was in use as a florist shop when photographed in September 2006. (Keith Fenwick)

In the late 1890s, the Highland built several stations in wood, such as Plockton. The T-shaped building included a large open veranda on the platform side with the booking office at the back. Similar designs were used on the Black Isle stations and at Burghead and Hopeman. When this view was taken the building was in use as a café, June 1993. (Keith Fenwick)

Aviemore was rebuilt when the direct line to Inverness was opened in the late 1890s in contemporary wooden style but with generous provision of awnings, which have recently been restored. Not that the awnings bring much comfort; it can still be a cold place when the wind blows. This view is looking north, with the main building on the left. The island platform on the right allowed trains from the Forres line to run into the station before being combined with the portion which had left Inverness later and come via the direct line. Nowadays it is the terminus of the Strathspey Railway. (J.L. Stevenson)

Grandtully was the only intermediate station on the Aberfeldy branch until the halt at Balnaguard was opened by the LMS in 1935. It was graced with a simple wooden structure. The right-hand portion, in horizontal lapboarding, was original. The left-hand end, in vertical beaded planking, has been added to provide extra storage. (Keith Fenwick)

Drybridge was one of the stations on the Keith to Portessie line, always referred to as the Buckie branch. It closed during the First World War and was prepared for a reopening which never happened in the 1920s. As part of that work the track was relaid and this station renamed Letterfourie. The simple shelter was a standard Highland design. (HRS Collection)

Four Highland stations were rebuilt by BR, one of them twice. The frontage at Inverness was rebuilt in the 1960s and is now in need of attention again. Lochluichart had a new station when the line was moved for the adjacent hydro scheme. A completely new building was erected at Forres in contemporary style in the mid-1950s. This is shown above in 1998. A section of original platform awning had been retained to its right to provide protection for passengers, but that was removed shortly after this photograph was taken. The Dava line platform was behind the left-hand half of the building and retained an awning until closure. (Keith Fenwick)

As an economy measure during the 1930s, the LMS and LNER stations at Elgin were combined and the ex-Highland building fell out of use; it was demolished in the 1960s. However, after the GNSR lines to Elgin were closed in 1968, the building was far too large and in the wrong place, so a new building was erected on the site of the Highland one. It is seen here in 1973. With a flat roof and typical cheap construction of the day, it lasted only about twenty years and was replaced by the present larger building in 1990. (Keith Fenwick)

Most Highland goods sheds were wooden. Size varied according to the location, but many were of similar size to the two illustrated here. One track ran through the shed, served by a platform inside capable of handling three or four wagons. Some had hipped roofs, as in Blair Atholl above, while others had gabled roofs. Brora is illustrated below; it is a listed building, as is Nairn, which has been moved to the Caledonian Railway at Brechin. Time has taken its toll on most of the other ones, including Blair Atholl, and they have been taken down. (Keith Fenwick above, Simon de Souza below)

9

BRIDGES AND VIADUCTS

Viaducts were a feature of the Highland, not surprising given the nature of the country it traversed. The routes of the earlier lines were carefully chosen to avoid crossing valleys, but estuaries on the coastal routes could not be avoided, as well as river crossings inland. The Nairn to Keith line had to contend with two substantial river crossings, over the Findhorn near Forres and the Spey near Orton.

The Perth line had several river crossings to make, notably over the Tay just outside Dalguise. The most difficult part was the Pass of Killiecankie which required a viaduct to carry the line past a precipitous section of rock as well as a tunnel, one of only two on the Highland Railway.

The Far North also had to contend with several rivers. The River Ness was crossed just north of the station at Inverness on a three-arch stone viaduct which was swept away by floods in 1989 and replaced by a modern concrete structure. North of Tain, the line took a circuitous route inland via Lairg to avoid crossing the Dornoch Firth. Even so, the Oykell Bridge at Culrain was a substantial structure. In the 1980s, a road bridge was built over the Dornoch Firth and plans were prepared to include a railway. This would have continued via Dornoch and used the trackbed of the Dornoch branch to rejoin the line at The Mound, saving thirty to forty-five minutes on the journey to Wick and Thurso. The investment required was not considered worthwhile and the plans dropped.

The Kyle line followed natural glens to the west so avoided any major engineering works to reach Strome Ferry. The extension to Kyle required a lot of blasting but no major bridges.

It was the direct line from Aviemore to Inverness which saw the most spectacular viaducts as well as a wooden trestle bridge on the boggy moor near Tomatin.

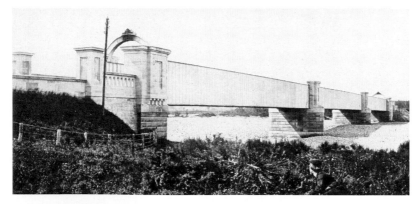

The River Findhorn bridge was just to the west of Forres and was constructed as an inverted 'U' with three spans of 150ft. The Spey bridge near Orton was of the same design, but had a single span of 235ft and was designed for double track. Great doubt was thrown on the adequacy of its design by the Board of Trade inspector, who required additional strengthening. It was rebuilt in the early twentieth century as a Pratt Truss. (HRS collection)

The Divie viaduct, just south of Dunphail station, was one of the more substantial structures on the original line to Perth. High up on the moors, it could be a bleak place in winter. Set into the inside of the parapet walls at the centre of the bridge are two plaques commemorating its opening and listing the original directors of the I&PJ. Today, the bridge is well maintained and can be used by walkers and cyclists as part of the Dava Way, which runs from Forres to Grantown using for the most part the trackbed of the railway. (Keith Fenwick)

At the Pass of Killiecrankie the river ran in a deep gorge, with the road climbing high above it. Both a viaduct and a tunnel were necessary for the railway. The views in Victorian times were more spectacular than can be seen today, as the trees have grown taller. (Author's collection)

North of Blair Atholl, the railway heads towards Druimuachdar summit. Near Struan, the route involves not only crossing the river but also the older road bridge over the same river. The original railway bridge was in stone, but when the line was doubled, a steel truss bridge was built. It can just be seen below the centre arch and completely ruins the view from the other side. (Norris Forrest/GNSRA)

The direct line between Aviemore and Inverness, built in the 1890s, had to contend with some steep gradients at each end, but there was a fairly level section near Tomatin across boggy moorland. This led to the construction of a wooden trestle, known as Altnaslanach viaduct, seen here in the 1960s. It was recently rebuilt and a concrete frame was inserted inside the original timberwork. (HRS collection)

Both stone and steel were used for viaducts on the direct line from Aviemore to Inverness. This is the largest, at Culloden, built entirely of stone. Culloden Moor station is just to the left of the viaduct, while the south end curves to the right as the line tackles the climb to Slochd. (Author's collection)

The slender and lofty Findhorn viaduct over the River Findhorn is just to the north of Tomatin station and is formed of steel spans on stone pillars. This is the view from the present A9 looking west, with the old road bridge over the river in the far distance. (Keith Fenwick)

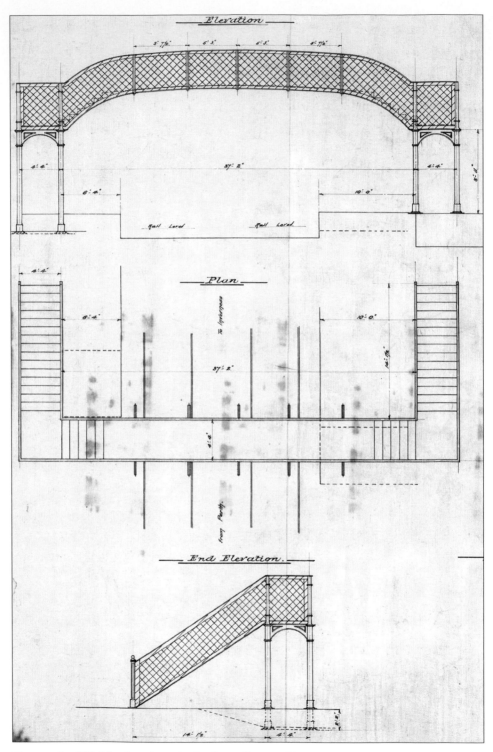

The standard Highland Railway footbridge is illustrated by these plans for the one at Murthly. Many were built at the Rose Street Foundry in Inverness. (HRS collection)

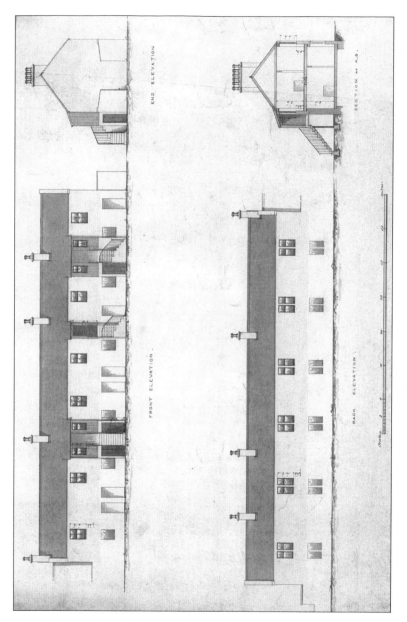

The plan for workmen's houses at Blair Athole (as it was spelt at that time).
On the ground floor there were six apartments, each with an entrance
lobby, main room and two small bedrooms at the back. On the first floor
there were four more identical apartments, plus a larger one with three
bedrooms at the left end. (HRS collection)

Most Highland loops were too long for the points at both ends to be operated from the same signal box, so a box was provided at each end. Above is the classic configuration of two boxes at Achnasheen, but in this case the West box, in the foreground, was east of the booking office. The East box can be seen in the distance. The down home signal in the distance also carries a distant signal for the West box. The up starter in the foreground was controlled by both boxes and protected the sidings on the left, July 1969. (Keith Fenwick)

Signalling equipment was supplied by both Duttons and McKenzie & Holland. The up starter at Elgin shows the large characteristic McKenzie & Holland finials. (D.L.G. Hunter)

10

SIGNALLING

The lines of the Highland Railway were built with the full knowledge that traffic would never be heavy; single lines were adequate and, in any case, all that could be afforded. For the Kyle and Far North lines, two or three trains a day met the demand, but further south traffic grew to such an extent that more and more passing places had to be added. Powers to double the line south of Aviemore were obtained in 1897 and renewed periodically until 1935, but the Highland could only finance the steepest section, from Blair Atholl to Dalwhinnie.

Originally the lines were worked to a strict timetable plus the use of the telegraph to signal trains from one station to the next. Any out of course running had to be specifically authorised by telegram from Inverness. This method was used without any mishaps for many years, but the Highland had to introduce tablet working after 1889 to comply with the new safety legislation. At the same time full signalling and the interlocking of points and signals had to be introduced at each passing place.

As with many other aspects of the Highland Railway, its signalling was quite individual. Tall signal posts capped with elaborate McKenzie & Holland finials, signal wires which ran overhead on posts to avoid being affected by snow and ice, tablet instruments in the booking office; these were all part of the scene.

When interlocking was installed, many passing loops were too long to be operated from one signal box. The Board of Trade would not allow long runs of points' rodding. So most loops had a signal box at each end. The tablet instruments were therefore placed in the booking office; this was a convenient central point, but also meant that the stationmaster remained in control and it was not necessary to employ fully qualified signalmen; lower-paid pointsmen would do. When trains crossed, the stationmaster could work one box and the pointsman the other – another example where Highland ingenuity led to economical working.

To ensure that proper control could be exercised from the booking office, the normal arrangement was that starting signals were controlled both by the box at the end of the loop next to the signal and from a lever in the booking office.

Highland practice was to stop most trains at all stations but on the main line the mail train in particular only served the more important ones. By the 1890s faster services were operated, especially to handle the peak summer traffic. Slowing down almost to a stop at each station to exchange tablets did not help, so drivers were in the habit of running too fast, resulting in firemen and signalmen suffering injuries from the heavy brass tablets and the iron hoop used to carry them. Fortunately, a solution came to hand from the GNSR, where James Manson introduced an exchanging apparatus which could be used safely at speeds of up to 60mph. Manson did not patent the design because he knew it could save lives, so the Highland was able to adopt it without paying royalties. This apparatus survived in use until the 1970s.

The LMS replaced tablet instruments with key token instruments on alternate single line sections as a safety measure. The physical difference gave the driver something that was quickly recognisable. The hoops and the pouches for the automatic apparatus were modified accordingly. While Highland regulations referred to 'tablet' working, terminology later changed to 'token' working.

Apart from the replacement of lower quadrant arms with upper quadrant ones in LMS and BR days, little else changed until the late 1960s.

There was a proposal as part of the 1955 modernisation plan to completely resignal the main line from Perth to Inverness using Centralised Traffic Control, a technology pioneered in America for long single line routes. Planning got underway, but then it was realised that the technology of the day was not up to the task given the number of passing places involved and the traffic on the line; it would take so long for the commands to signals and points to be transmitted and acknowledged that the traffic could not be handled successfully.

By the late 1960s, something had to be done on the main line. Several local stations had closed, commercial pressure demanded faster train speeds but the auto changer proved less reliable on diesel engines due to their different springing. The answer was tokenless block. Track circuits were used to detect trains entering and leaving single line sections; these were interlocked with the starting (now section) signals which became the authority to the driver to proceed. This system has worked successfully ever since. Inverness itself has been fully resignalled and remote operation of some loops introduced.

On the line to Aberdeen, tokenless block was also installed between Elgin and Keith, as well as east of Keith, but tokens are still in use between Elgin and Nairn, with track circuit block thence to Inverness.

North of Inverness, radio tokenless block was introduced in the mid-1980s, controlled from Inverness. This provided the type of centralised traffic control which was planned for the main line

in 1955. Apart from the swing bridge over the Caledonian Canal at Clachnaharry, trains run on their own north of Inverness. The radio receiver in the cab gives a visual indication to the driver of his authority to enter a single line section. Points are sprung to direct trains into each loop but have to be passed at limited speed. The Train Protection and Warning System has since been added to provide greater safety, although this requires trains to run through loops at a lower speed. About twenty minutes has been added to the journey time to Wick as a result.

Left: Murthly box was an example of one of the McKenzie & Holland boxes. It was actually situated originally at Millburn Junction, one of four boxes installed in 1898 at Inverness and had, for the Highland, unusually decorative barge boards. The box still stands and is listed, but out of use for many years, it now looks in poor condition. (Keith Fenwick)

Left, below: Dalraddy, photographed in September 1937, was a passing loop on the main line between Kincraig and Aviemore, provided in 1910 when additional capacity was needed. This design, used from about 1876, was the most common on the Highland. The loop was closed by the LMS, only to be reopened during the Second World War, when a brick box was installed. (J.L. Stevenson)

Forres required three signal boxes, one at each apex of the triangle. This is the West box during BR days. It is typical of the larger style, which was required at more complex locations. The wooden stand on the left was used by the signalman for manual token exchange. (HRS collection)

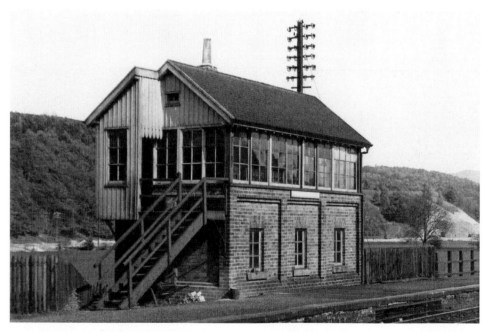

From 1900, a Highland design using mainly brick construction was introduced and this was continued until the grouping. Rather than plain brick walls, the bases were 'panelled' as shown here at Ballinluig. (Author's collection)

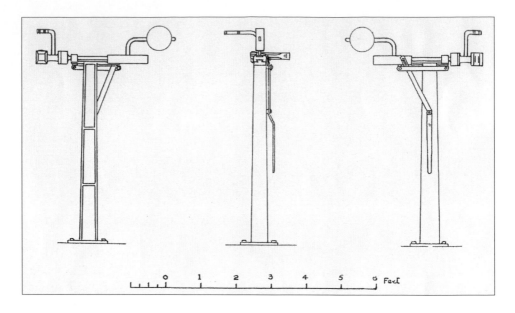

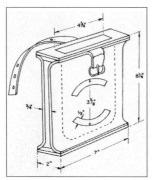

A technical drawing of the tablet catcher stand by Sir Eric Hutchinson (above), which originally appeared in *Model Railway Constructor*. The signalman pulled the lever by the column away from the track to push the catcher forward when the train was approaching. The catcher was detachable and normally kept in an adjacent wooden cabinet for safety.
The catcher stand had to be located at a precise distance from the track, so was not installed where there was any cant on the track. A portable gauge which was placed on the rails was used to periodically check the alignment of track and stand. The leather holder for the tablet is illustrated on the left and shown below. (Simon de Souza)

There was no problem in manual token exchange at Clachnaharry as trains were limited to 5mph over the swing bridge, which the box also controlled. The driver of a northbound train in August 1969 has just received the token for the section to Lentran and the signalman has the one from Inverness firmly around his arm. Electric Token working north of Inverness continued until Radio Tokenless Block was introduced in the mid-1980s. It survives today on two sections, Elgin to Forres and Forres to Nairn. (Keith Fenwick)

An eastbound train entering Achanalt, a bleak crossing point on the Kyle line, in the 1950s. The driver is about to give up the token to the signalwoman but she does not have one to give to the driver so the train must be going to either cross or shunt the sidings. Even so, the dangers of manual token exchanging can be imagined. (Cumbrian Railways Association)

Moy had a curious piece of apparatus to hold the tablet changer in the form of a heavy base which ran on tracks out to the platform edge. Accurate end stops would be needed to ensure that the catcher was precisely placed in relation to the track. (Courtesy Anthony Lambert)

While the automatic apparatus was very successful on steam engines where the body sat on a solid chassis, diesel locomotive bogies were well sprung so the body tended to bounce more. Token exchange failures grew. Trains had to come to a sudden stop and drivers and signalmen had to search through the undergrowth to retrieve the lost token. The introduction of tokenless block on the main line in the late 1960s largely eliminated these problems. Here, in August 1969, the token which should have been collected from a southbound train at Muir of Ord North box can be seen a couple of feet up in the air. The bay platform for Fortrose trains was behind the lamp-post. (Keith Fenwick)

The apparatus fitted to a class 25 diesel was located in a recess below the cab side window, just in front of the door. The driver had to reach out of the window to load and retrieve the token. (Keith Fenwick)

When the Swindon three-car diesel units were introduced on the Aberdeen to Inverness run in 1960, tokens had to be exchanged at several points between Keith and Dalcross, so automatic catchers were fitted. The only suitable place was in the guard's area; the guard was then responsible for exchanging tokens. By the early 1970s most of the crossing places had been eliminated. DMUs picked up at Elgin West (above) and exchanged at Forres, where the loop is inconveniently sited outside the station. The fitting on the diesel is shown right. A recess was made in the side of the coach but its limited room meant that the spring holding the token to be dropped off had to be hinged. A wooden panel behind the catcher enabled the guard to load it. After exchange he had to retrieve the new token from the jaws on the left before checking it and confirming by special bell signal to the driver that he had authorisation to be in the section. (Keith Fenwick)

Nairn was the last station to retain two signal boxes and it had a very long loop. In recent years, only one member of staff has been on duty at a time, so a bicycle was provided to enable him or her to get between the booking office, where the token instruments were located, and the two boxes. Here the signalman returns with the staff as an eastbound special waits to cross. This practice came to an end in 2000, when colour light signals and power-operated points were introduced. (Keith Fenwick)

Two new signal boxes were provided in the 1950s. A traditionally designed one at Gollanfield and a modern brick structure with concrete roof at Grantown-on-Spey, in both cases replacing two boxes. This one barely survived for ten years before the line was closed. (HRS collection)

11

DEALING WITH THE ELEMENTS

Highlanders expect snow in winter and are generally prepared for it, but the early railway builders did not realise just how difficult it would be to keep the trains running in adverse conditions. Cuttings were the problem; they could easily fill up with snow if the wind was blowing in the wrong direction. Railwaymen soon came to know the danger points and take precautions, but often it was impossible to stop snow building up.

One of the earliest examples of a snow plough was claimed by the Morayshire Railway in 1854. To combat drifts on the line, its locomotive superintendent, Joseph Taylor, came up with a design in the shape of a wedge about 2ft high covered with canvas.

Early experience on the Perth line showed that something much more substantial was needed. Various designs evolved. Small ploughs which could be fitted throughout the winter months were carried by many engines while much larger ones were kept ready to tackle serious problems. Diesel locomotives could not support large ploughs, but were equipped with small ones in front of the leading wheels. Independent ploughs were designed and a snow blower was purchased to clear the deepest cuttings. However, some recent winters have been quite mild, so these have seen limited use.

It was not just snow that caused problems. Twice in the early years of the twentieth century, summer thunderstorms struck with such concentrated force that part of the line between Aviemore and Slochd was washed away, in the first instance causing loss of life. Floods in 1989 washed away the River Ness viaduct at Inverness and the line to Elgin and Keith has been damaged on several occasions.

Small Goods class 2-4-0 No. 21 in Barclay's dark green livery has been fitted with a big plough. This locomotive's boiler exploded in 1872, after which the loco was rebuilt, so this photograph must have been taken before 1872. The plough was secured to the locomotive above the buffer beam, with additional stays to the frame by the leading axlebox, and was kept fitted to the loco during the winter months, preventing the loco from doing other work. (F. Moore)

One can almost feel the cold in this view of a Barney 0-6-0 No. 17695 with a medium-sized snow plough at Blair Atholl in the 1930s. These would be used to keep the line clear where no major snow blocks had built up. (J.L. Stevenson)

Even a slight covering of snow could cause problems. This is the line at Druimuachdar blocked in the early 1960s. A double-headed northbound train is waiting for the line to be cleared. A Black Five sits a little further along the line and in the distance a southbound train is waiting. The main road to Inverness runs on the right, close to the electricity pylons. (HRS collection)

Independent Snow Plough ADB965198 was at Inverness in June 1973. An independent unit was needed once diesels came on the scene and several were constructed using the chassis of old tenders. The three axles of this one can be seen in the protrusions on the skirting. Behind the tender, the class 25 is equipped with small ploughs in front of each wheel; these were enough to deflect light accumulations. (Keith Fenwick)

Class 158s operating from Inverness now incorporate a neat design of plough extending across the front of the vehicle and painted in yellow to match the rest of the front end. 158 740 is leaving Keith on a train for Inverness, 27 August 2006. (Ron Smith)

Blockages from snow were relatively infrequent, but snow fell regularly. It could jam points and signal wires; in many places the wires were carried on posts several feet above ground. This is a typical winter afternoon in February 1969 as a northbound freight enters Aviemore. The short day is already drawing to a close, and the temperature is falling. It had been 0°F (−17°C) the previous night, so cold that the heating in the morning train to Inverness did not work and the windows were frozen on the inside. (Keith Fenwick)

At several places, snowdrifts could easily block the railway and many miles of line, especially north of Helmsdale, were protected by snow fences such as this example near Forsinard. Constructed out of old sleepers, they were rough and ready affairs which in recent years have not been maintained. At certain particularly vulnerable places, snow blowers – high angled wooden platforms at each side of the line – were built to avoid snow building up in cuttings. (Howard Geddes)

12

SOME HIGHLAND SURVIVORS

W ith so much of the original mileage still open, it is not surprising that there is still a taste of the old Highland to be seen, chiefly in the station buildings, bridges and viaducts that have survived for upwards of 150 years.

On the modern railway, apart from Inverness, only Pitlochry, Kingussie, Aviemore, Nairn, Forres, Elgin, Dingwall, Wick, Thurso and Kyle are staffed, and then some for only part of the day. The large buildings at these stations, several of which have listed status, have to be maintained. Only the modern building at Elgin is ideally suited to current needs. At other stations, commercial uses have been sought for the spare accommodation but it is not always easy to find tenants. Many of the other extant station buildings have been sold off as houses. Achnasheen has become a bunk house for backpackers, while Kyle of Lochalsh houses a gift shop, small museum and a restaurant. At Pitlochry a voluntary group runs a bookshop in part of the station, while the smaller building at Nairn houses a colourful florist's shop.

To celebrate the centenary of the formation of the Highland Railway in 1965, the Scottish Region arranged for No. 103 to work special trains between Inverness and Forres for a week. Here it waits to leave Inverness on one of these workings, hauling two preserved Caledonian Railway coaches. (Norris Forrest/GNSRA)

One Highland locomotive and two coaches survive in preservation, and the Strathspey Railway keeps steam active in the Highlands on the line from Aviemore to Broomhill.

Fortunately the LMS put aside No. 103, the first of the Jones Big Goods and the first 4-6-0 in the British Isles, when it was withdrawn in 1935 and, even more fortunately, it survived the drive for scrap metal during the Second World War. The loco was kept at St Rollox in Glasgow, but in a bid to provide publicity, was put back into service in 1959 by British Railways, along with three other pre-grouping locos. It was used over the next six years on occasional special trains but retired again in 1965. Nowadays No. 103 can be seen in the Glasgow Transport Museum.

The other locomotive associated with the Highland, although never owned by the company, is the 0-4-4T built for the Duke of Sutherland by Sharp Stewart but designed by David Jones. The Duke had the right to run his own locomotive between Inverness and Dunrobin, a right which continued throughout LMS days although that company was not really sure whether it had legally passed on from the Highland at the grouping. With the formation of BR, the use of the locomotive ceased and it was sold and spent some years at New Romney in Kent. It was sold again in 1965 and transported to Canada. It can now be seen at Fort Collins in British Columbia, along with the four-wheeled coach which was built for journeys between Dunrobin and Inverness. The Duke of Sutherland, who was also a director of the L&NWR, had a bogie saloon built by that company for longer journeys; this is now in the national collection at York. It was the precursor of clerestory-roofed L&NWR and WCJS eight and twelve-wheeled stock built in the first few years of the twentieth century.

Although a few Highland coaches survived into the 1950s, only two have been preserved. One is a composite six-wheeler and the other is a four-wheeled brake which for many years provided shelter at Inchlea, one of the bleakest spots on the main line over Druimuachdar. It had to be run along the line with broken springs when it was recovered because there was no road access at Inchlea. The composite will hopefully be a feature of the new museum in Glasgow. No Highland wagons survive.

No. 103 has just arrived in Dumfries in October 1965 on its final outing. The loco was given a fairly light load of three coaches, but was earlier seen racing up the steep gradient from Barrhead to Lugton on a wet Sunday morning in fine style. (Norris Forrest/GNSRA)

After the Dava line closed to all traffic in 1965, freight continued to run over the ex-GNSR line from Craigellachie through to Aviemore until November 1968. To mark its closure, a special was run from Aberdeen to Aviemore, calling at nearly all the stations including Boat of Garten. (Keith Fenwick)

The same place twenty-six years later as Caledonian Railway 0-6-0 No. 828 is ready to leave in July 1994 on a train for Aviemore. Caley 0-6-0s were known as Caley Barneys on the Highland. No. 828 was the star attraction on the Strathspey Railway for several years and will return after overhaul. (Keith Fenwick)

The Stathspey Railway started by purchasing the track from Aviemore to Boat of Garten in 1971, together with the trackbed on to Grantown-on-Spey. Passenger services started in July 1978, using a new terminus at Aviemore 500yds north of the main line station. This was created from scratch, using a building from Dalnaspidal. The buildings at Boat of Garten were restored. North of there, the track was relaid and the station at Broomhill recreated, to which place trains started working in May 2002. Regular steam-hauled services are provided throughout the tourist season. The line is currently being rebuilt to Grantown-on-Spey, but there are two major obstacles. A new bridge deck has been obtained to cross the River Dulnain, where the original piers still stand, but the narrow bridge over the A95 was removed many years ago and the road realigned. A completely new bridge will be needed here. At Grantown, the original station site is now occupied, so a new station will have to be built. At Aviemore, the railway has been able to extend into the main station, putting the buildings on the island platform to good use.

Many small items are to be found in both public and private collections. The Scottish Railway Museum at Bo'ness, the National Railway Museum at York, the Glasgow Transport Museum and Inverness Museum all display relics. The museum at Kidderminster beside the Severn Valley Railway station includes many signalling items. Some of the smaller museums in the Highlands have other items, such as Inverness & Nairn Railway lamp-posts at Nairn.

Paper records survive in the National Archives of Scotland, including all the Minute books, many drawings, etc. The Highland Council is actively developing its archive service and has featured railways on its website (www.ambaile.org.uk), with many photographs and drawings. For all those interested in the history of the line, the Highland Railway Society provides a regular magazine and meetings for researchers and modellers and has its own expanding archive of artefacts, drawings, photographs and other ephemera.

Station lighting could be quite rudimentary. On the left is a survivor at Boat of Garten on the Strathspey Railway, which originally housed a small paraffin burner but is now converted to electricity. Where town gas was available, that was used. Some gas lamps bore the inscription of the railway company; an Inverness & Nairn Railway from Nairn is illustrated on the right. When new station lighting was provided, these were moved to the museum in the town, where they can still be seen. (Keith Fenwick)

Above: The Strathspey Railway has been extended to Broomhill where the loop is beyond the station. The train, which is just visible on the right, is in the loop while the locomotive runs round; in this case it is BR 2-6-4T No. 80105 on loan from Bo'ness, September 2004. (Keith Fenwick)

Right: At Broomhill, a new station has been erected on the site of the old one in the style of a typical Highland Railway wooden building. Also installed is the double arm signal, although it is not an exact replica. Several wayside stations including Broomhill had such signals to indicate when a train had to stop. The present Broomhill has found fame as it featured as Glenbogle in the BBC TV series *Monarch of the Glen*. (Keith Fenwick)

Aviemore is still a busy station, but its facilities are far beyond what is needed today. As part of the town's development, a section of the road frontage has been rebuilt for commercial use but the building on the island platform was for many years empty and decaying. As a listed building, it was difficult to find any use for it. The answer came once agreement had been reached to extend the Strathspey Railway into the station from its previous terminus to the north. At the same time, funding was obtained to restore and repaint the buildings. A new loop was built for the Strathspey trains, plus a new car park on the right. Services started in July 1998. (Keith Fenwick)

New signs have been provided, in Highland Railway style, but in common with other stations throughout the Highlands and with a nod to the tourist, the name is also shown in Gaelic, even though Gaelic was never used by the Highland Railway. (Keith Fenwick)

Footbridges on the Highland were generally of lattice construction, most of them from the Rose Street Foundry at Inverness. Similar structures were to be seen throughout Scotland. Several of these survive in use and have been refurbished by being dismantled and shot blasted to remove a century or more's worth of paint and grime before being reassembled and painted. This is Tain, after renewal, in September 2006, painted in purple/blue and white. Local effort has added to the tidiness and colour of the station. (Keith Fenwick)

Lybster was at the end of the branch which came south along the coast from Wick, and therefore the furthest point on the railway network from London. The line opened in 1903 and closed in 1944. The building has now found a new use as the nineteenth hole on the local golf course. (Keith Fenwick)

Above: The great thing about wooden buildings was that they could be moved. This happened to several signal boxes and some station buildings. This is the former up platform shelter at Achnashellach, relocated to the side of the road through the village. The railway is a short distance up the hill on the left. (Keith Fenwick)

Left: Water towers had to contend with severe winter conditions. Water was carried up a central pipe which was surrounded by an outer column. The air in the gap between them could be heated by a small fire, the housing for which can be seen near the foot of the column. There were several holes for the smoke to escape – in full working order on a freezing cold day these columns must have been quite a sight with smoke and steam pouring out all around. This one at Altnabreac survived long after it was last used simply because the station was so isolated it was difficult to remove it. (D.L.G. Hunter/HRS collection)

Sourcing sleepers long enough to support both sets of rails at points was a problem in pre-grouping days. Standard length sleepers were used instead, interlaced to support each set of rails separately. All have been replaced, except this one at Helmsdale, photographed in June 1992 but still in place in 2008. (Keith Fenwick)

Highland minimalism is illustrated in the simple design of this wicket gate at Strathpeffer. (Simon de Souza)

Although there have been no regular steam workings over any of the Highland lines such as operate between Fort William and Mallaig, several specials have been run over the years, often at the end of the Mallaig line operating season. In October 1997, class 4 4-6-0 No. 75014 worked from Inverness to Kyle of Lochalsh to celebrate the centenary of the line. The loco had to make the return journey tender first and stopped at Achnasheen for a bit of attention. The loco uncoupled from the train so that the firebox could be cleaned out and water taken from a road tanker. (Keith Fenwick)

Duncraig is the station after Strome Ferry and close to Plockton on the Kyle line. It consists of a short platform and this delightful shelter, and was built to serve Duncraig castle, the home of the Matheson family. The platform was officially closed in 1964 but reopened in 1976 as the castle, which looks more like a country house, housed a domestic science college at that time. It was empty for a while after that, and then housed the crew on the popular BBC TV series *Hamish Macbeth*. An extended family has since bought the castle. (Keith Fenwick)

There is a strong interest in modelling among enthusiasts of the Highland Railway. Sir Eric Hutchinson was a prominent modeller; his articles in the *Model Railway News* in the 1950s provide a wealth of prototype detail. James Kennedy created a Gauge 1 layout in his garden in Inverness and built superb locomotives and rolling stock to

run on it. After his death, some of the models found a new home at Inverness Museum. Several others were purchased by the Kennedy Trust, set up by local enthusiasts to ensure that as much of the collection as possible remained intact and in the Highlands. These are brought out at exhibitions and shows. Durn was one of the locomotives working on the short exhibition layout at Nairn Museum in July 2005 as part of the Inverness & Nairn 150th anniversary celebrations. (Keith Fenwick)

The bridge which carried the Aberfeldy branch over the River Tay near Ballinluig is now owned by the local community and has been converted, through their efforts, to a road bridge. This is the scene on a spring morning in 2006. (Keith Fenwick)

Stanier class 8 2-8-0s were not associated with the Highland, although they regularly worked between Perth and Inverness during the Second World War and did reach the far north on at least one occasion. Since then, the only other known visit was No. 48151 *Gauge O Guild* on a railtour in 1998. The train set out from Inverness on a Saturday morning but poor coal led to delays, the train eventually reaching Thurso late in the evening, when even the chip shop had run out of fish. On Sunday, the train worked back south and has stopped at Forsinard (above) in sunshine and strong wind; few trees grow in that part of Scotland since the wind never seems to stop blowing. (Keith Fenwick)

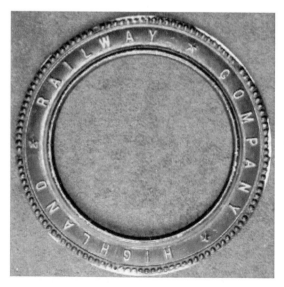

Many smaller items of Highland interest survive and there are even some replica items, such as cap badges, made to appear genuine. The item illustrated here led to some head scratching when it was first seen. It appeared to be a genuine artefact and was one of several identical ones seen. Some 12in in diameter in cast iron, it was eventually determined that it was fixed to the underside of the carriage roof around the oil lamp hole. (Ray Nolton)

13

INTO THE TWENTY-FIRST CENTURY

When Dr Beeching set out his plans in the *Reshaping of British Railways* over forty years ago, not many journeys in the Highlands were made by rail on a daily basis. School children were carried to the nearest school if train times permitted, but few people commuted into Inverness to work. Local bus services were more convenient for most people, but rail still dominated for longer distances.

Today much has changed. The railway's value to the local community and the tourist industry is well recognised. The future is a political question, but it would be a bold politician who suggested any reduction of the present facilities.

Inverness is now a city, one of the fastest growing places in the country. Despite new access roads and a bridge over the Beauly Firth, traffic congestion is becoming a problem. The town provides employment for a much wider area, so rail services are expanding once again. Regular commuter trains bring workers into Inverness every day from as far away as Lairg. Four services are provided on both the Far North and Kyle lines throughout the year and there is also a Sunday service on both these routes.

Inverness station has been gradually modernised over the years. Resignalling in the 1980s was accompanied by simplification of the trackwork, but the basic layout was retained. The roof has been rebuilt. In August 2008, a class 158 waits to leave on an Aberdeen working while the class 67 which has brought in the overnight sleeper is berthed in platform 1 on the left. In the distance, another 158 is boarding passengers for the Far North line. (Keith Fenwick)

Nos 37100 and 37430 leaving Keith for Inverness, 29 September 1995. The train consisted of freight for Wick and Thurso plus empty log wagons. This was the first freight to the Far North for fifteen years. At that time, there was regular timber traffic at various stations on the Aberdeen to Inverness line but no freight at all was worked over the Highland main line. Containers such as those seen here were in any case prohibited until work took place in Kingswood tunnel to improve clearance. (A.G. Murdoch/GNSRA)

On the main line to the south, rail offers a convenient way to travel to Edinburgh or Glasgow and back in a day and the service has steadily been improved. Weekly traffic flows have developed. Sunday evening services on the Far North line are among the busiest as people return south for the week's work or study.

Much of the credit for this is due to the Highland Rail Partnership, which is now part of HITRANS, the Highlands and Islands Transport Partnership. A full-time officer is able to identify new traffic needs and work to satisfy them. Its efforts have resulted in new commuter services for Inverness, under the banner of 'Invernet'. This has been so popular that there is now the problem of providing enough capacity to satisfy demand. User groups for both the Far North and Kyle line have also been set up as voluntary organisations. The Friends of the Far North has kept the spotlight on that line and worked towards improvements in its passenger service.

Freight has presented the railways with more of a challenge. With a long haul up the ever more congested A9, it might be thought that rail would have a distinct advantage. Despite much encouragement through the availability of grants to set up facilities and the efforts of the Highland Rail Partnership, rail has gained few regular traffic flows. For a time traffic did increase, with regular shipments of foodstuffs and parcels, but it was not possible to retain these flows. Timber has been carried in some quantity, but that market is cyclic, depending on where the timber has to be felled. Rail is caught by catch-22; it only works economically when there is plenty of traffic, but it is difficult to achieve critical mass. However, with the increasing cost of fuel, new flows have been identified and new facilities are being set up in Inverness. A new intermodal service carrying food started in late 2008 as part of a well-integrated operation with road collection and delivery at each end.

Reducing journey time is key to ensuring continued increase in passenger traffic. This means more investment to improve track alignment and signalling. An hourly service to the south would be very attractive and has been promised by 2012, as quicker access to the central belt of Scotland is now seen by politicians as a necessity. The current signalling on the Far North line will soon be life expired and restricts train speed. Bit by bit, these problems are being tackled to ensure that the railway lives on in the Highlands.

Container shipments for the grocery chain Safeway were operated to Inverness for a few years and used the stub of the harbour branch to unload there. However, this traffic disappeared after Safeway was taken over by Morrisons, as its distribution depot in central Scotland was not rail connected. (Keith Fenwick)

Safeway also had a store in Wick, so it was a natural extension to carry that traffic by rail. A transhipment point was set up at Georgemas. In turn, a local white goods factory was able to make use of this facility to carry goods south. A good example of the economics of scale, but once the Safeway traffic disappeared, so did the transport of white goods. The taxpayer has not received a good return on the amount invested in the hardstanding. (Mark G. Lyons)

It is now over 150 years since the first parts of the Highland Railway were opened and these anniversaries have been marked locally, starting with celebrations in Nairn in 2005. Although the actual anniversary was in November, the event took place in July to get the benefit of better weather. Many of the guests travelled from Inverness on the mid-morning train on a class 158 unit. At Nairn, a commemorative plaque was unveiled and then the procession made its way through the town to the museum to enjoy lunch. (Keith Fenwick)

Many local stations on the Far North line were closed in 1960, but with the growth of Inverness in recent years there is now steady commuter traffic. Alness and Muir of Ord reopened using the original platforms, but reopening Beauly proved more difficult, as the track had been realigned and the building and station approach were in private use. The solution was a platform on the west side of the line, but finance could only be found for a short one. Selective door operation had to be introduced to ensure that passengers only used the centre doors in the two-car units. A northbound train enters the station in July 2005. (Keith Fenwick)

Since 1989, an HST has provided a daytime working between Inverness and London. On a fine morning, with the hills a deep brown and just a hint of snow on the tops, the southbound working approaches the summit at Druimuachdar, late November 2003. The speed limit in this area varies between 90 and 100mph. The service is now operated by National Express East Coast. (Mark G. Lyons)

Class 67 No. 67030 waits to leave Inverness with the southbound sleeper service, while in the adjacent platform the daytime *Highland Chieftain* has arrived from London Kings Cross, June 2003. These two trains carry on the tradition of providing direct links between the Highlands and England. (Keith Fenwick)

A southbound freight train runs through the loop at Slochd Mhuic, 'pigs den', in June 2001. The summit here is 1,315ft high, a bit lower than Druimuachdar, but it is a 22-mile climb up from sea level at Inverness. The train consists mainly of empty cement wagons returning from Inverness. To the right is the original A9 and further right the modern road, here as in many places, just single carriageway. Despite being rebuilt in the 1980s, this road is very busy, making rail travel an attractive alternative. (Mark G. Lyons)

It is still possible to photograph a train from the classic viewpoint at Kyle of Lochalsh, but the railway is being gradually squeezed in by development of parts of the pier which are no longer required for railway use. Logs are stacked along the pier, waiting to be loaded onto a German freighter in this view taken in September 2007. (Keith Fenwick)

A southbound First ScotRail class 170 approaches the summit at Druimuachdar, with the hills all around shrouded in mist, March 2008. Imagine this journey in early Highland days with no heating. (Keith Fenwick)

In late 2008, a new regular intermodal service started between Grangemouth and Inverness operated by Stobart Rail. This is the southbound train near Tomatin, hauled by 66427. Both the locomotive and the containers were in smart blue livery, January 2009. (Mark G. Lyons)

BIBLIOGRAPHY

An extensive range of books has been published about the Highland Railway and various parts of it. The list below shows those which are believed to be in print or readily available on the second-hand market, but is by no means exhaustive.

Cormack and Stevenson *Highland Railway Locomotives*, Books 1 and 2 (RCTS, 1988)

Dawson, Ian K. *Findhorn Railway* (Oakwood Press)

Geddes, Howard and Bellass, Eddie *Highland Railway Liveries* (Pendragon, 1995)

Fenwick, Keith *Inverness & Nairn Railway* (Highland Railway Society, 2005)

Fenwick, Keith *Railways of Keith* (GNSRA, 2006)

Fenwick, Keith and Sinclair, Neil T. *Inverness & Aberdeen Junction Railway* (Highland Railway Society, 2008)

Fenwick, Keith and Sinclair, Neil T. *Perth & Dunkeld Railway* (Highland Railway Society, 2006)

Fenwick, Keith, Sinclair, Neil T. and Ardern, Richard J. *Lost Stations on the Far North Line* (Highland Railway Society, 2010)

Fletcher, Peter, *Directors, Dilemmas and Debt* (Highland Railway Society, 2009)

Hamilton Ellis, C. *Highland Engines and Their Work* (Locomotive Publishing Co., 1930)

Hawkins, Reeve and Stevenson *LMS Engine Sheds* Volume 6 (Irwell Press 1989)

Hunter, D.L.G. *Carriages and Wagons of the Highland Railway* (Turntable Enterprises, 1971)

'JEC' (John Edgar Campbell) *Iron Track through the Highlands* (Highland News, 1923)

Jenkinson, David *Highland in LMS Days* (Pendragon, 2004)

King, Lilian *Last Station: The Story of Dalnaspidal* (1997)

King, Lilian *Railway Childhood* (1997)

Lambert, Anthony J. *Highland Railway Album* Volume 1 (Ian Allan, 1974)

Lambert, Anthony J. *Highland Railway Album* Volume 2 (Ian Allan, 1978)

McConnell, David *Rails to Kyle of Lochalsh* (Oakwood Press, 1997)

McConnell, David *Rails to Wick & Thurso* (1990)

Malcolm, Eric H. *Cromarty & Dingwall Light Railway* (Cromarty Courthouse, 1993)

Nock, O.S. *Highland Railway* (Ian Allan, 1965)

Ross, David *Highland Railway* (Tempus, 2005)

Sinclair, Neil T. *Highland Main Line* (Atlantic Publishers, 1998)

Sinclair, Neil T. *Highland Railway: People and Places* (Breedon Books, 2005)

Stephenson Locomotive Society *Highland Railway, Its Constituents and Successors* (Stephenson Locomotive Society, 1955)

Thomas, John *Skye Railway* (House of Lochar)

Thomas, John and Turnock, David *Regional History of the Railways of Great Britain* Volume 15, North of Scotland (David St John Thomas)

Turner, Barry C. *Dornoch Light Railway* (2002)

Vallance, H.A. *History of the Highland Railway* updated by Clinker and Lambert as *The Highland Railway* (House of Lochar)

Wilkinson, Brian *The Heilan Line (Portessie branch)* (Dornoch Press, 1988)

More information can be found for the various organisations mentioned in the text from their websites:

ScotRail: www.scotrail.co.uk

Friends of the Far North Line: www.fofnl.org.uk

Friends of the Kyle Line: www.kylerailway.co.uk

Am Baile, the Highland Council's website: www.ambaile.org.uk

Highlands and Islands Transport Partnership (HITRANS): www.hitrans.org.uk

Highland Railway Society: www.hrsoc.org.uk

THE HIGHLAND RAILWAY SOCIETY

The Highland Railway Society caters for all those interested in the varied aspects of the railway, from its foundation to the present day. An illustrated quarterly journal is distributed to members and contains a wide variety of articles and information. Members' queries are a regular feature and details of new books, videos and models of interest are reported. A series of Occasional Papers enables specific topics to be covered in depth.

Meetings are held regularly in both Scotland and England. An annual gathering is held each September and includes a full day of talks, films etc., as well as an opportunity to meet fellow members.

The society has a library, and photographic and drawing collections which are available to members. Copies of drawings are available for purchase. Modellers are well catered for. Complete kits are produced in limited runs. Specially commissioned modelling components such as axle boxes, buffers and springs are available, plus a comprehensive set of transfers to enable any Highland loco to be named.

Membership details of the Highland Railway Society can be found on the Society's website: www.hrsoc.org.uk

Other titles published by The History Press

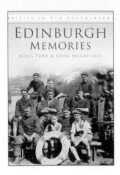

Edinburgh Memories
MILES TUBB & JOHN MCCAUGHIE

Edinburgh Memories is the unique and fascinating result of many conversations and interviews with local people, recalling life in their city between the two world wars. Vivid memories are recounted, including childhood and schooldays, work and play, sport and leisure. Everyone who knows Edinburgh, as a resident or a visitor, will be amused and entertained, surprised and moved by these stories, which capture the unique spirit of Scotland's capital city.

978 0 7905 5100 5

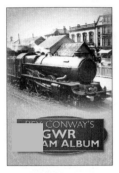

Rex Conway's GWR Steam Album
REX CONWAY

With over 250 photographs, this volume delves into the history of the GWR before 1948 – the year that British Railways came into existence following the nationalisation of the 'Big Four' railway companies. Here we see a plethora of engines such as 'Saints', 'Stars', 'Halls', 'Castles' 'Kings' and 'Bulldogs'. Featuring views of Swindon Works, Brunel's magnificent station at Bristol Temple Meads, halts, tunnels, sheds and bridges from Penzance to Paddington, this book is a must-have for everyone with a passion for the GWR and the golden age of steam.

978 0 7524 5153 4

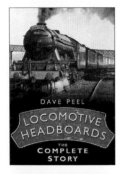

Locomotive Headboards: The Complete Story
DAVE PEEL

Researched over five years, this volume covers all named trains that ran with headboards from initial small-scale use, through the LNER's extensive usage in the 1930s, mass headboarding in the early BR period, to final decline. Differing designs and construction methods are examined in detail, while variations in shape and style are fully explored. Illustrated with over 400 photographs, this is an invaluable reference source for all railway historians, while railway modellers will also find it of great assistance.

978 0 7905 4462 5

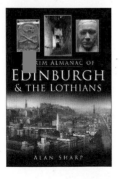

A Grim Almanac of Edinburgh & The Lothians
ALAN SHARP

Seldom in history has there been a city with a more sordid reputation than Edinburgh. Beneath the surface respectability of the jewel in the Scottish crown lies a warren of filth-ridden alleys and stairs where thieves, murderers and ghouls of every description planned and carried out their foul deeds. In this book we meet them all. Major Weir, the devil-worshipping black magician and his wicked sister Grizel; Deacon Brodie, the inspiration behind *Dr Jekyll and Mr Hyde*; and of course, worst of all, Mr Burke and Mr Hare, who plied their swift trade in corpses for the dissection table of Dr Knox.

978 0 7509 5105 0

Visit our website and discover thousands of other History Press books.
www.thehistorypress.co.uk